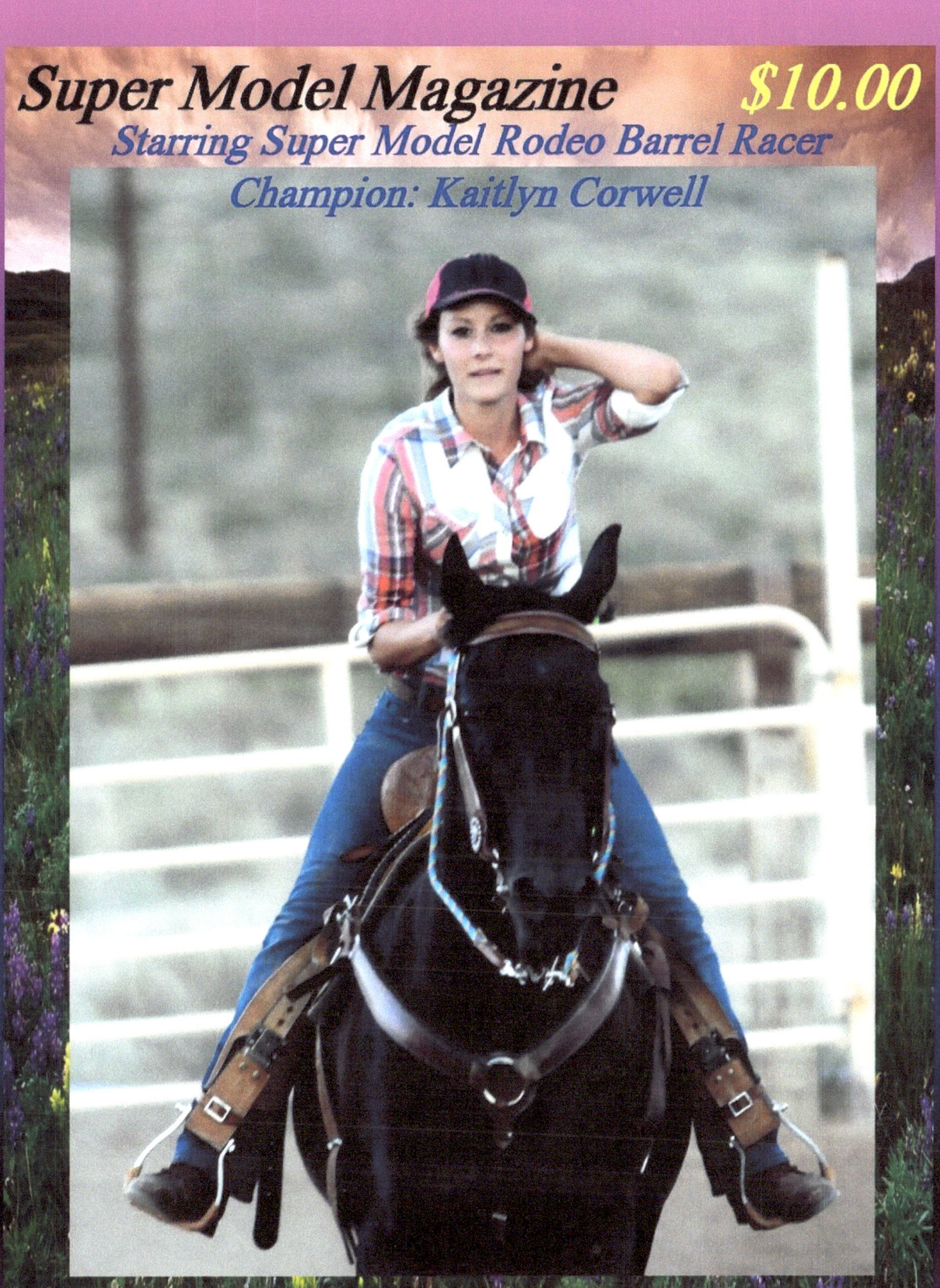

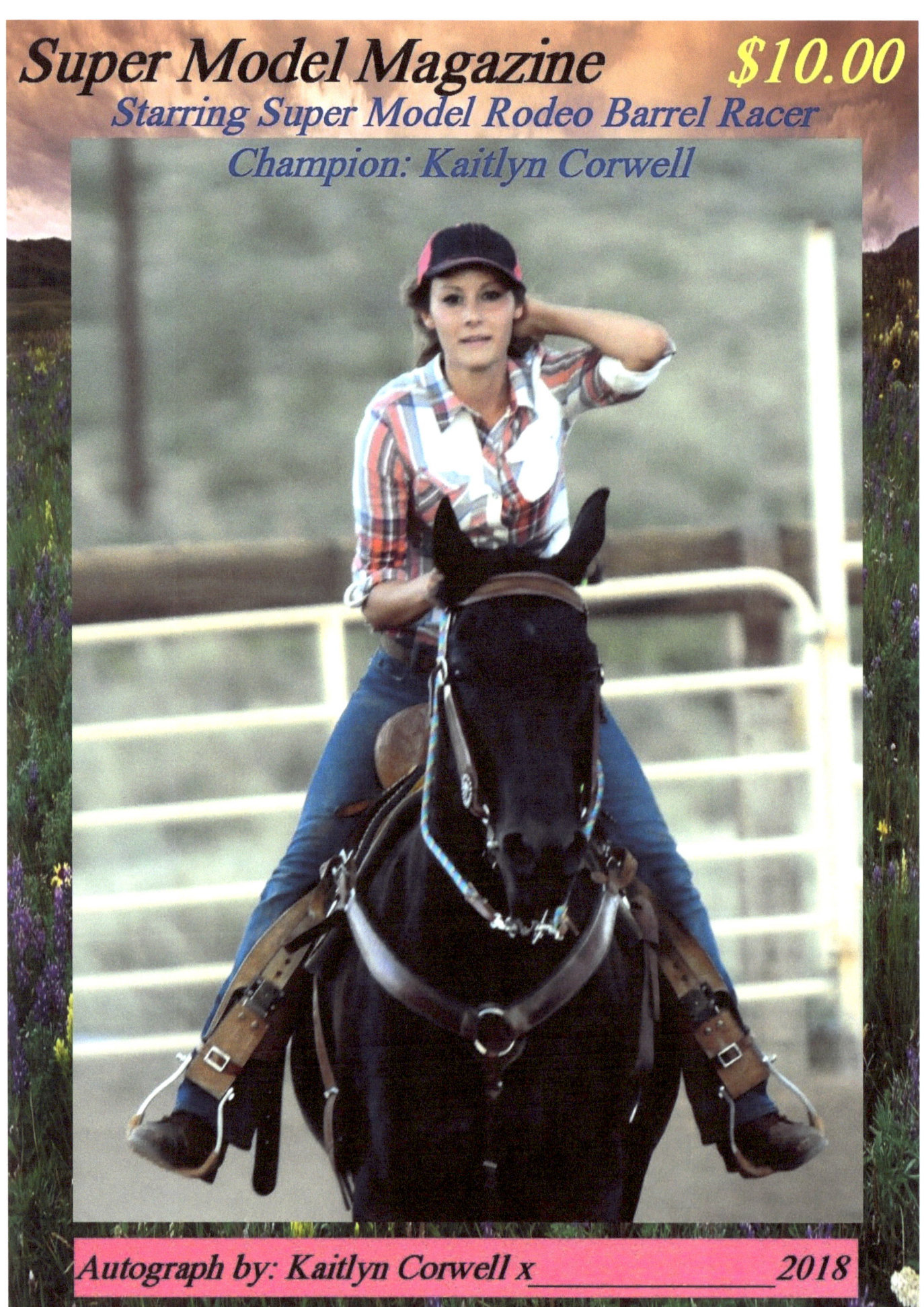

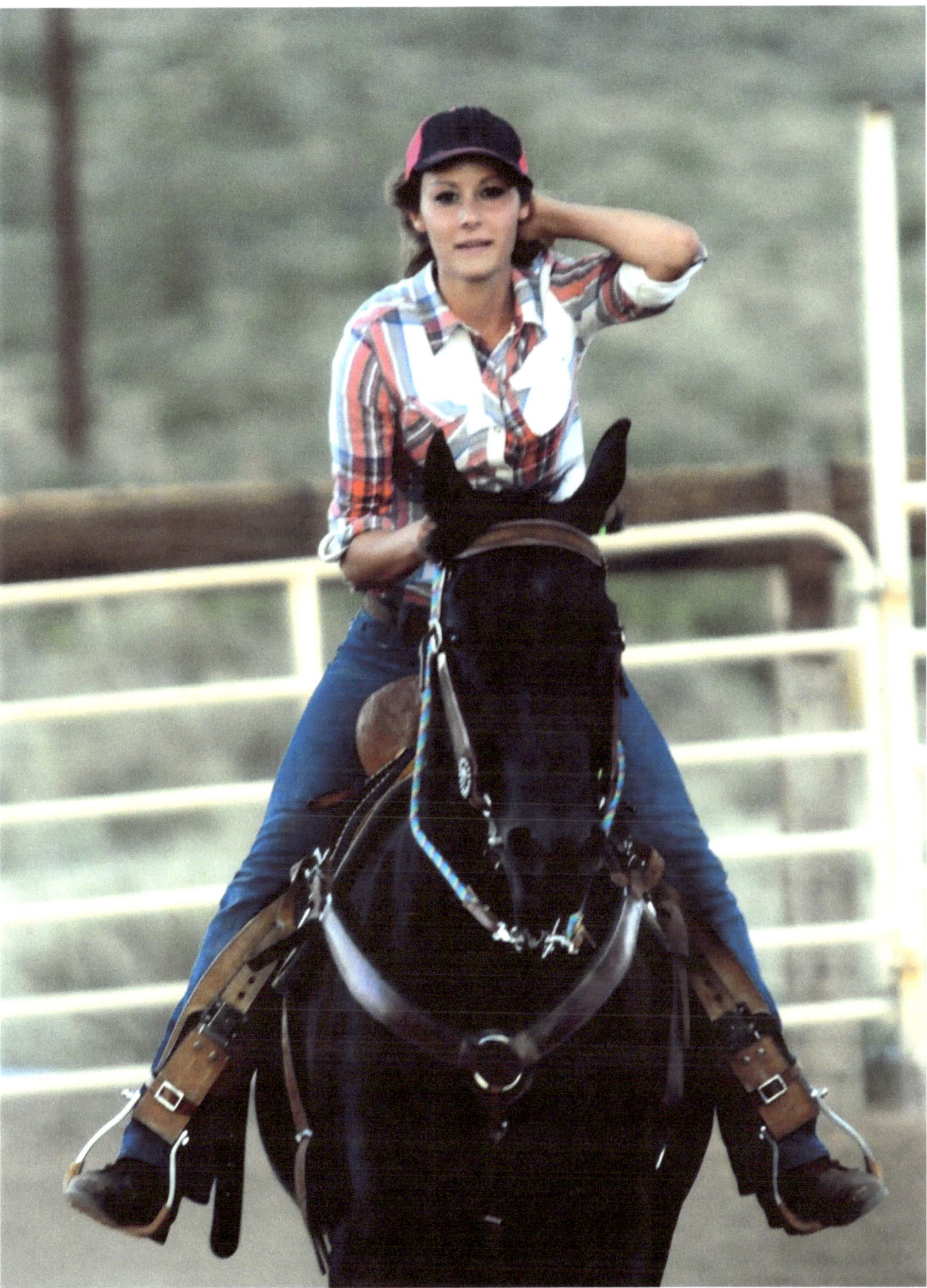

Super Model Magazine $10.00

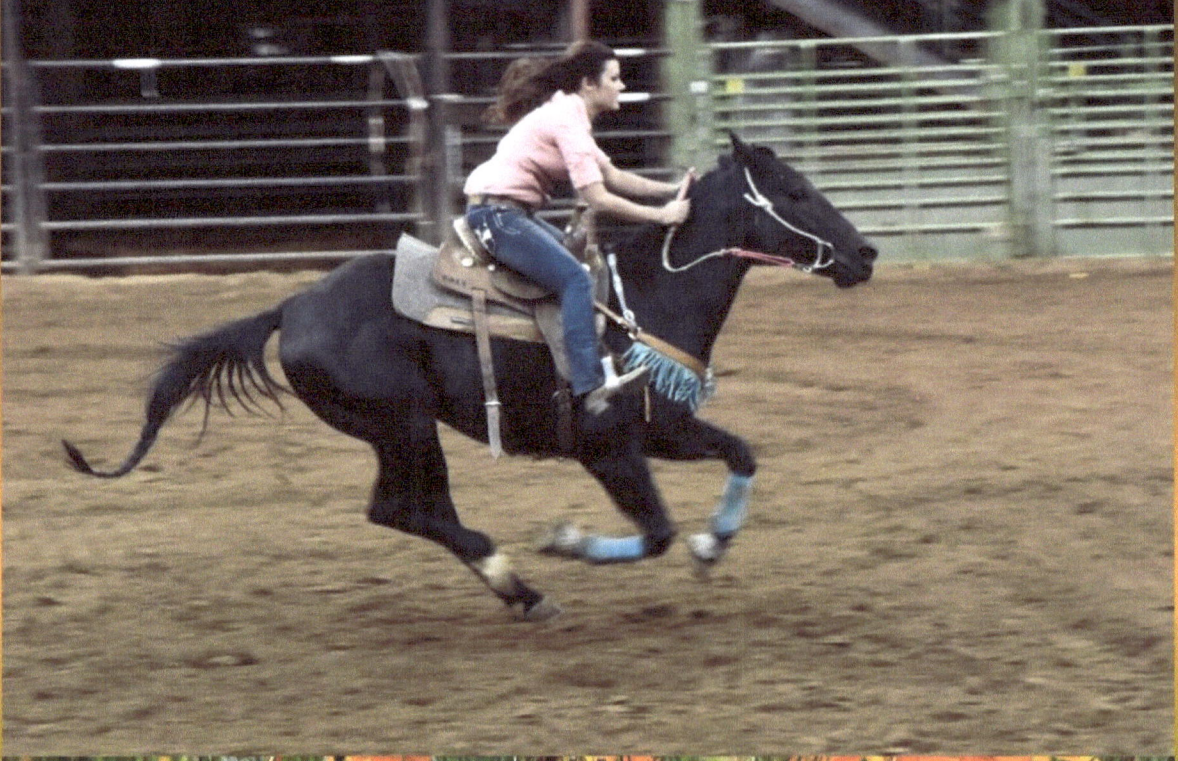

Debuting Super Model Rodeo Barrel Racing Champion: Kaitlyn Corwell

Signed by: Kaitlyn Corwell x_____ 2018

Ms. Kaitlyn is a world champion rodeo barrel racer. She loves animals and rides hard and fast on the track. She is the Danika of Horse Racing. dmp

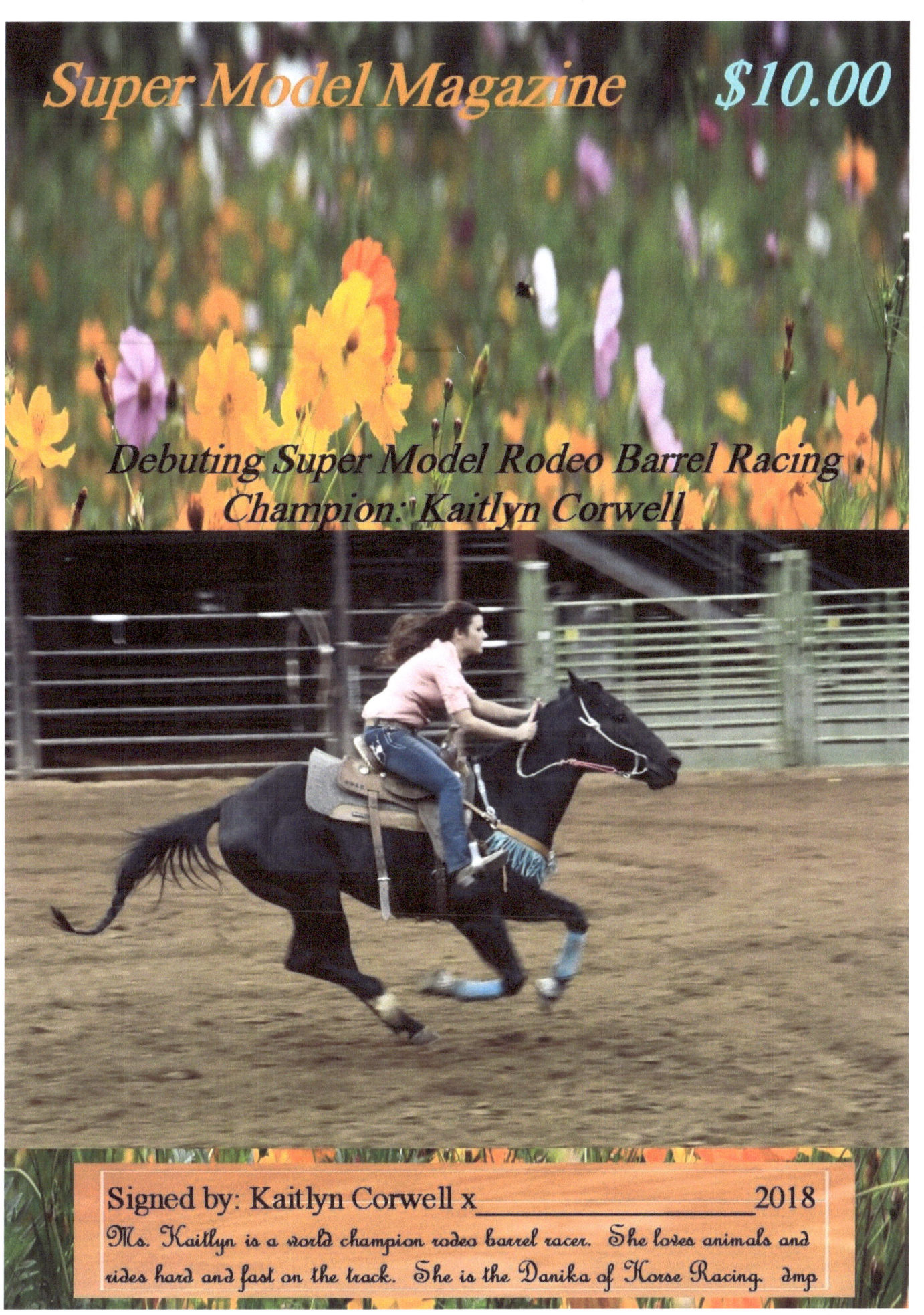

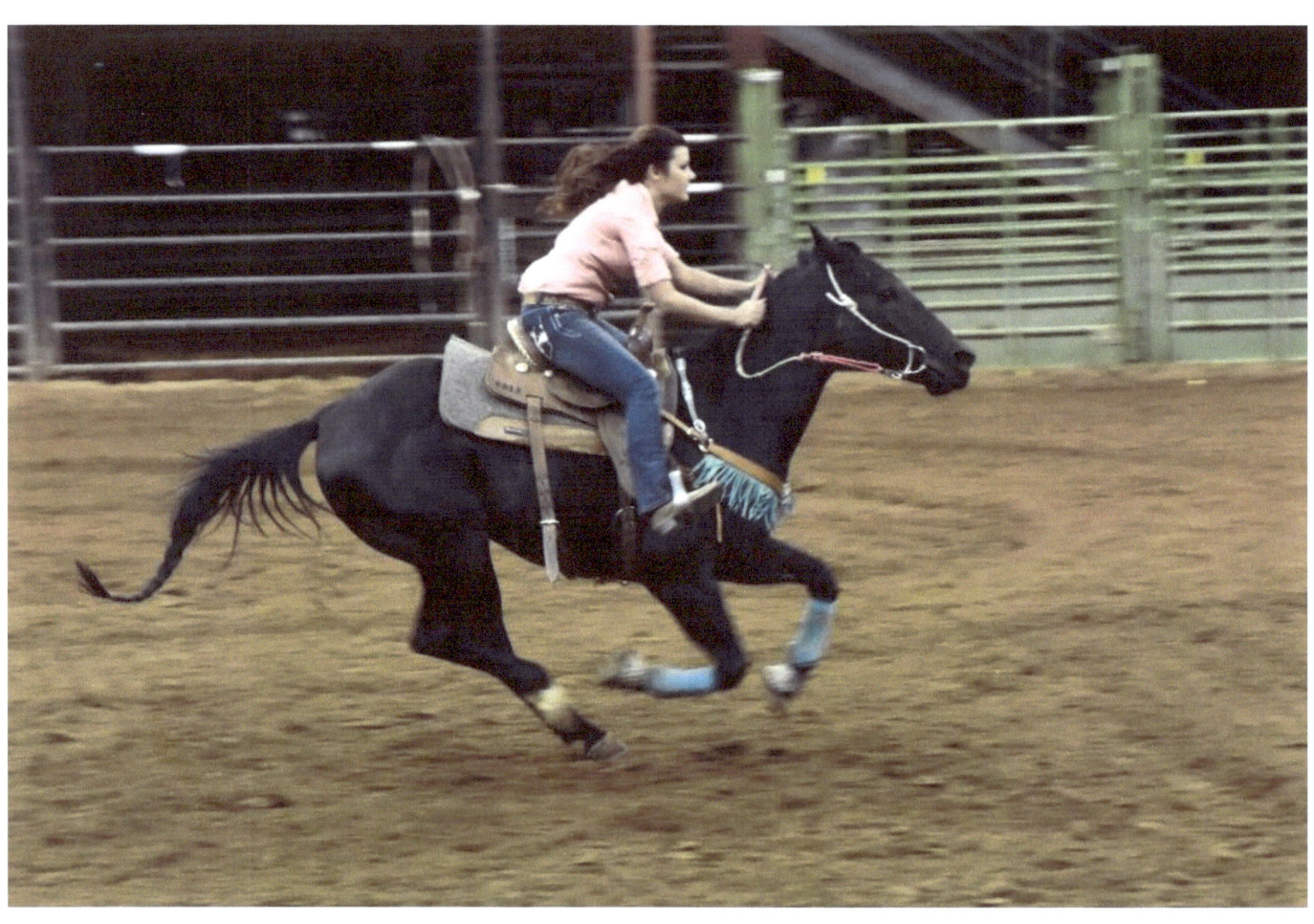

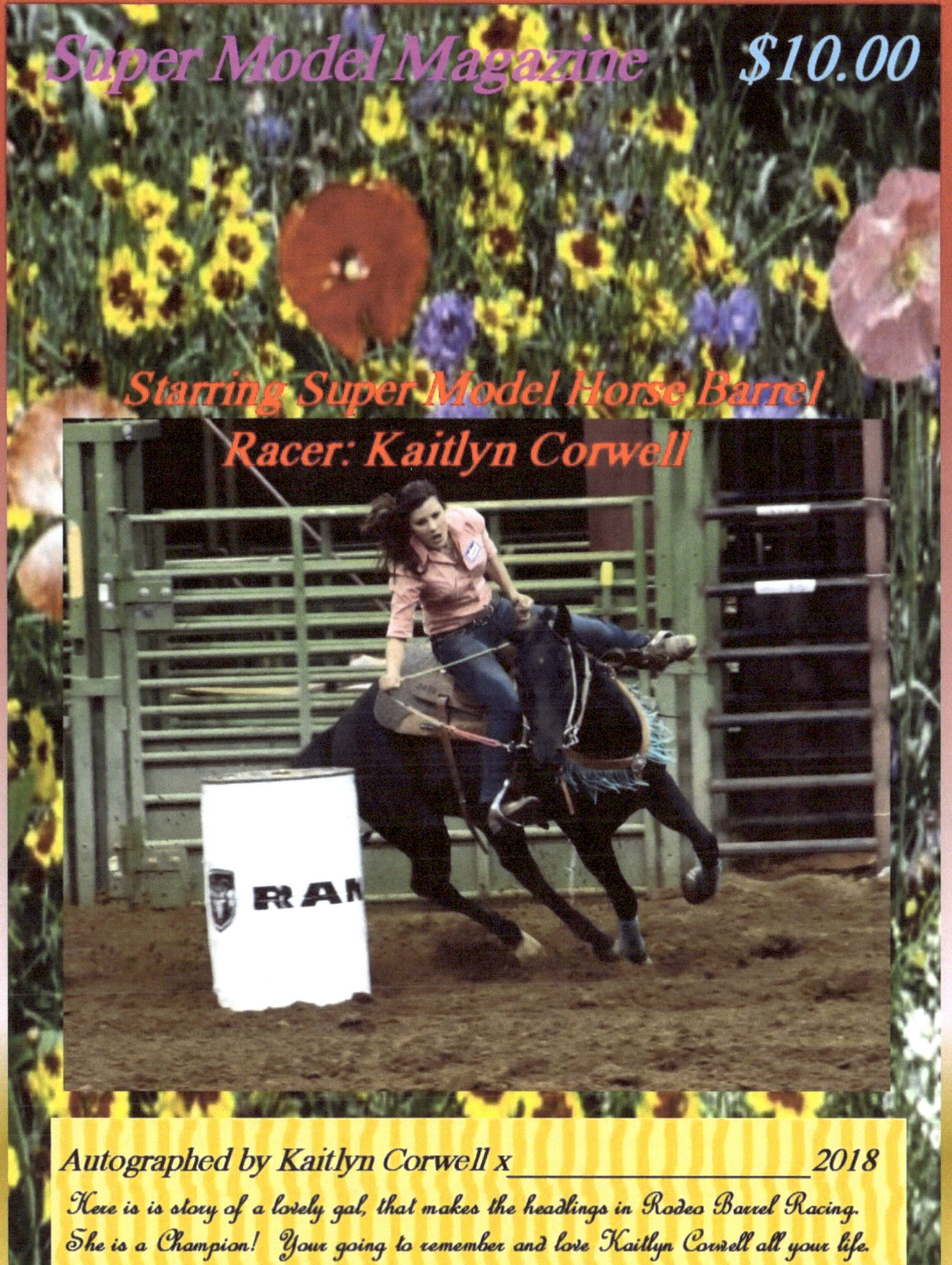

Super Model Magazine $10.00

Starring Super Model Horse Barrel Racer: Kaitlyn Corwell

Autographed by Kaitlyn Corwell x_____ 2018

Here is is story of a lovely gal, that makes the headlings in Rodeo Barrel Racing. She is a Champion! Your going to remember and love Kaitlyn Corwell all your life. Ride-Em Cowgirl, that is America's Newest Super Model of Finesse and Flair. dmp

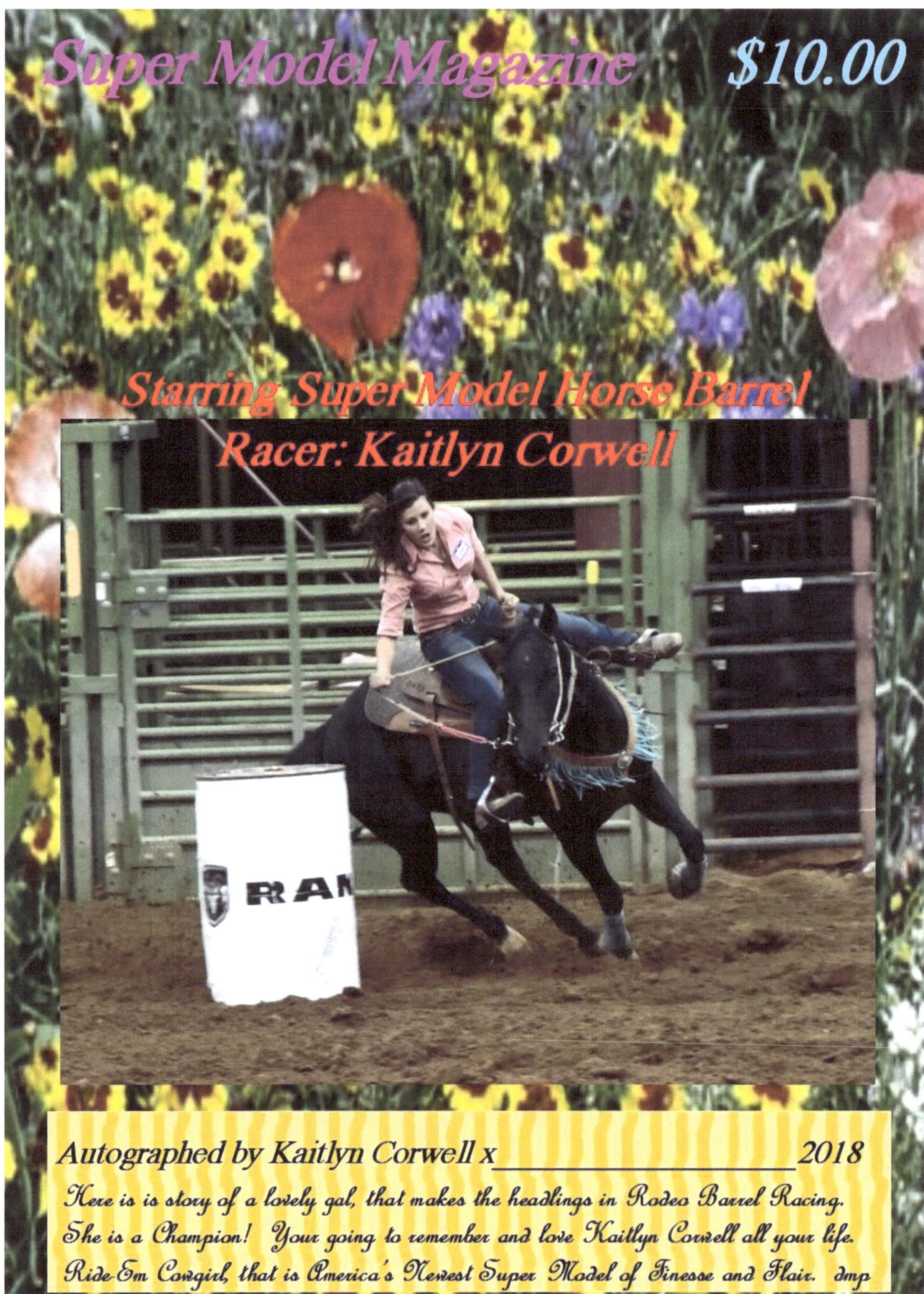

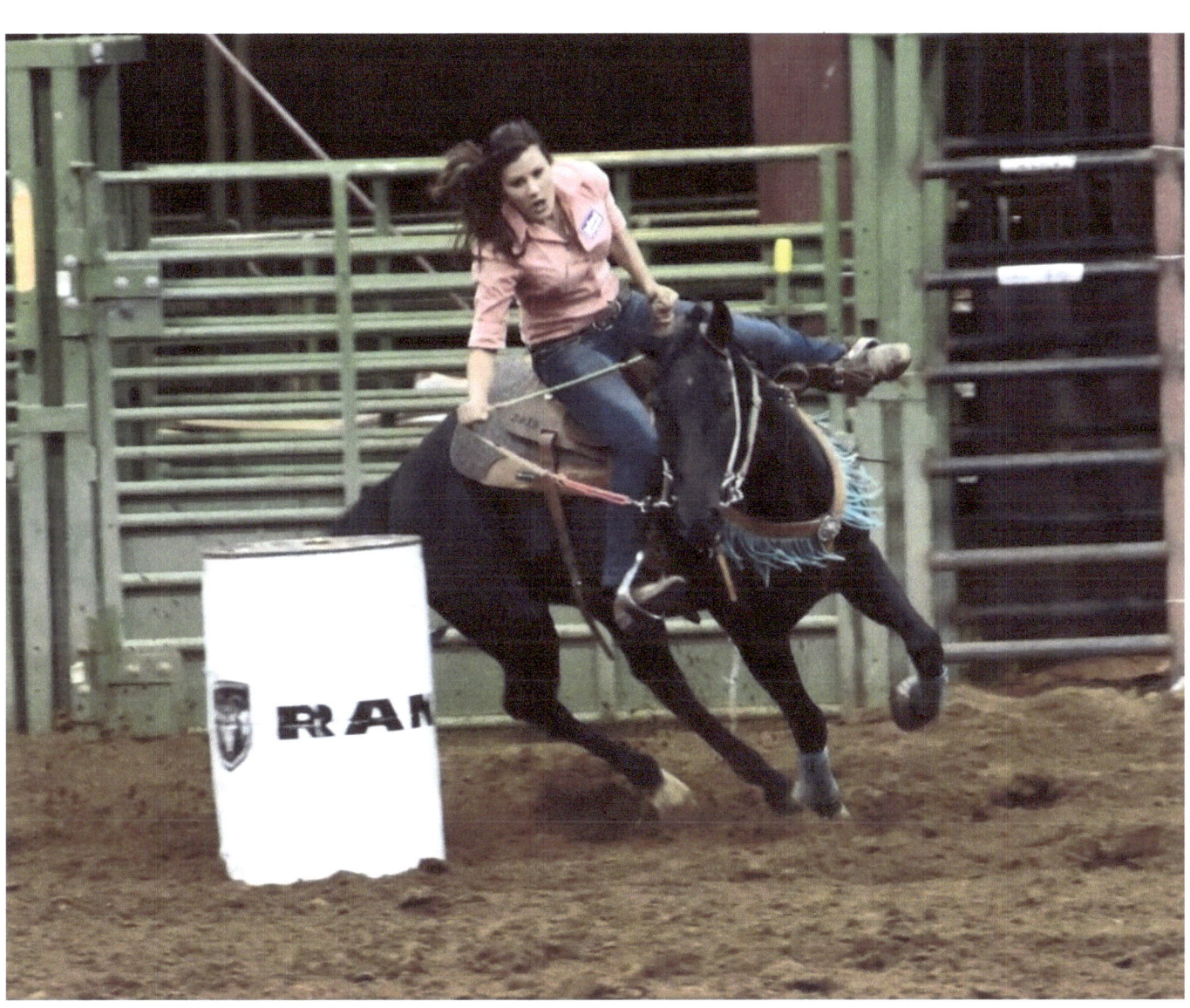

Super Model Magazine: $10.00

Starring Super Model Rodeo Barrel Racing Champion: Kaitlyn Corwell

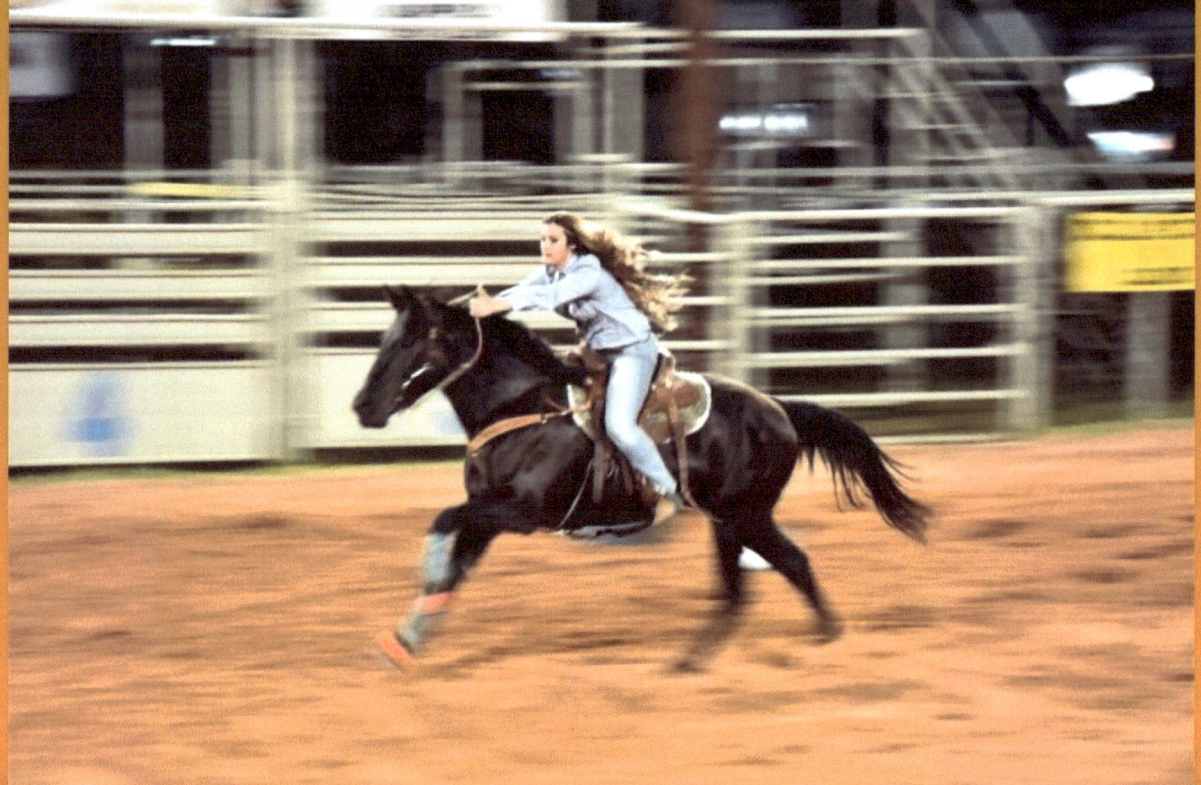

Autographed by: Kaitlyn Corwell x_____ 2018

Kaitlyn entertains as champion, much like found in the movies of a majestic ride. She is a Country Girl with a future in these United States of unsurpassing grace and charm. This young lady can thrill you and she's not horsing around. America wins with Kaitlyn Corwell

Super Model Magazine: $10.00

Starring Super Model Rodeo Barrel Racing Champion: Kaitlyn Corwell

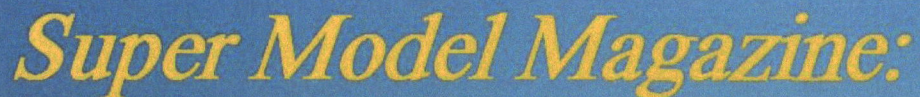

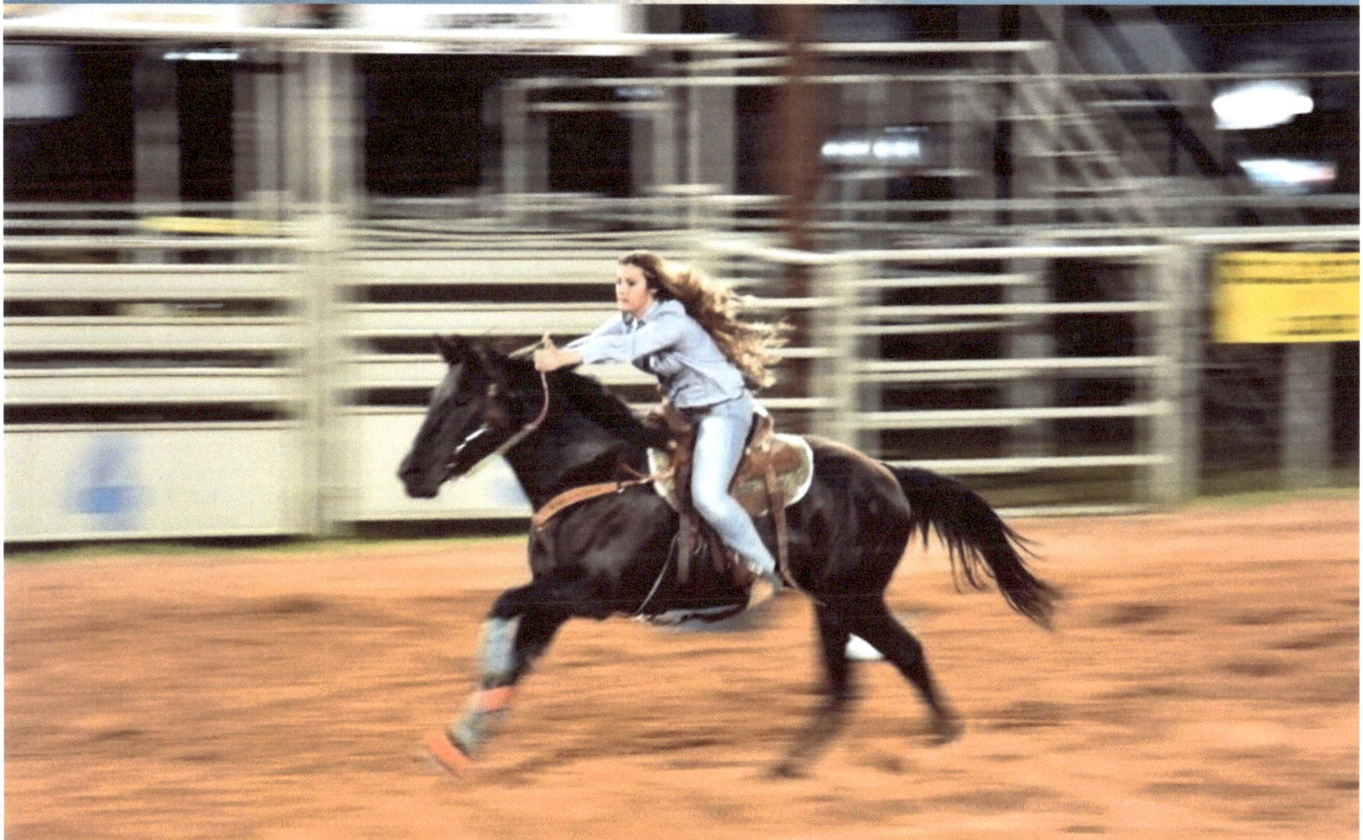

Autographed by: Kaitlyn Corwell x_____ 2018

Kaitlyn entertains as champion, much like found in the movies of a majestic ride. She is a Country Girl with a future in these United States of unsurpassing grace and charm. This young lady can thrill you and she's not horsing around. America wins with Kaitlyn Corwell

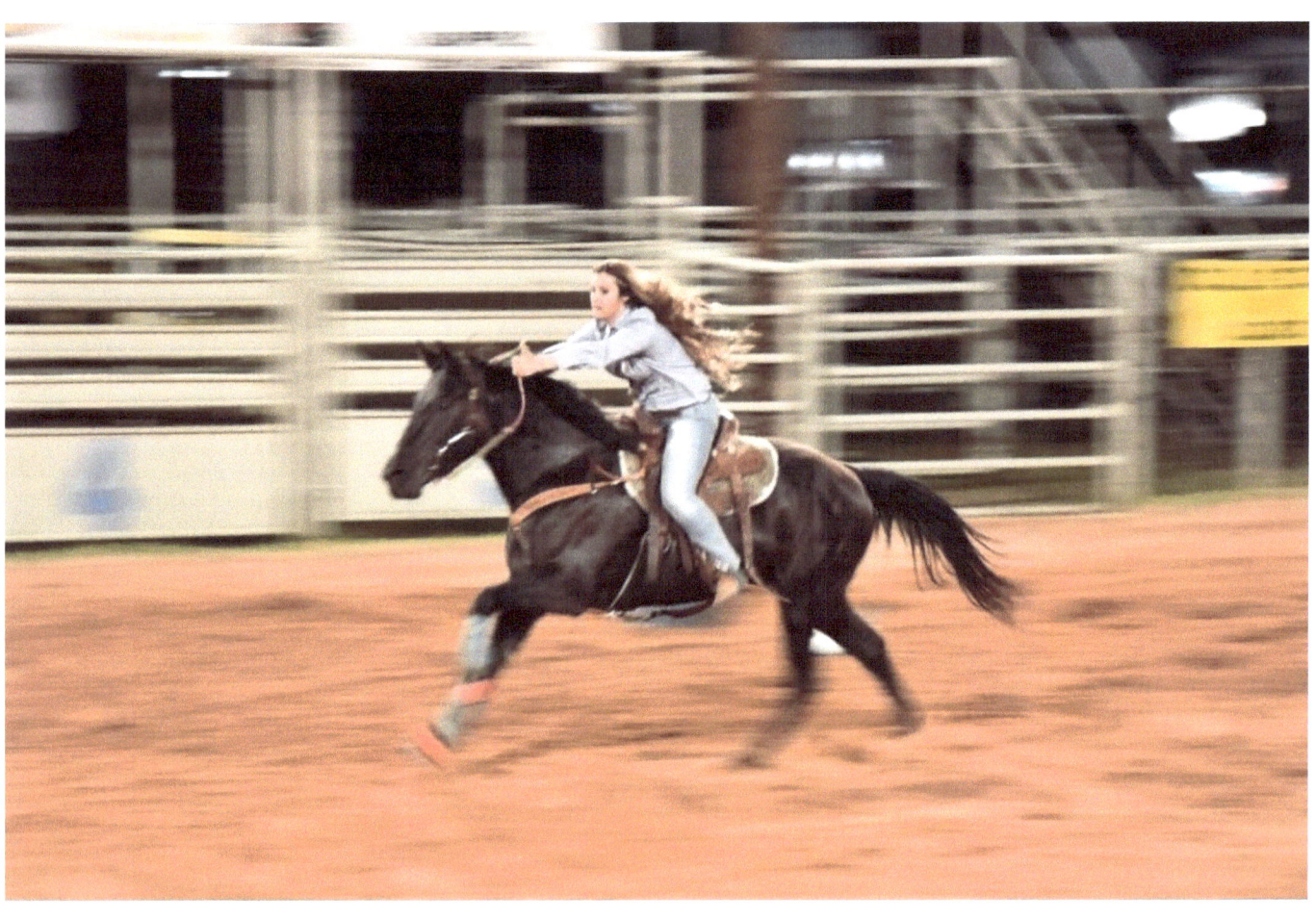

Super Model Magazine $10.00

Starring Super Model Rodeo Barrel Racer Champion: Kaitlyn Corwell

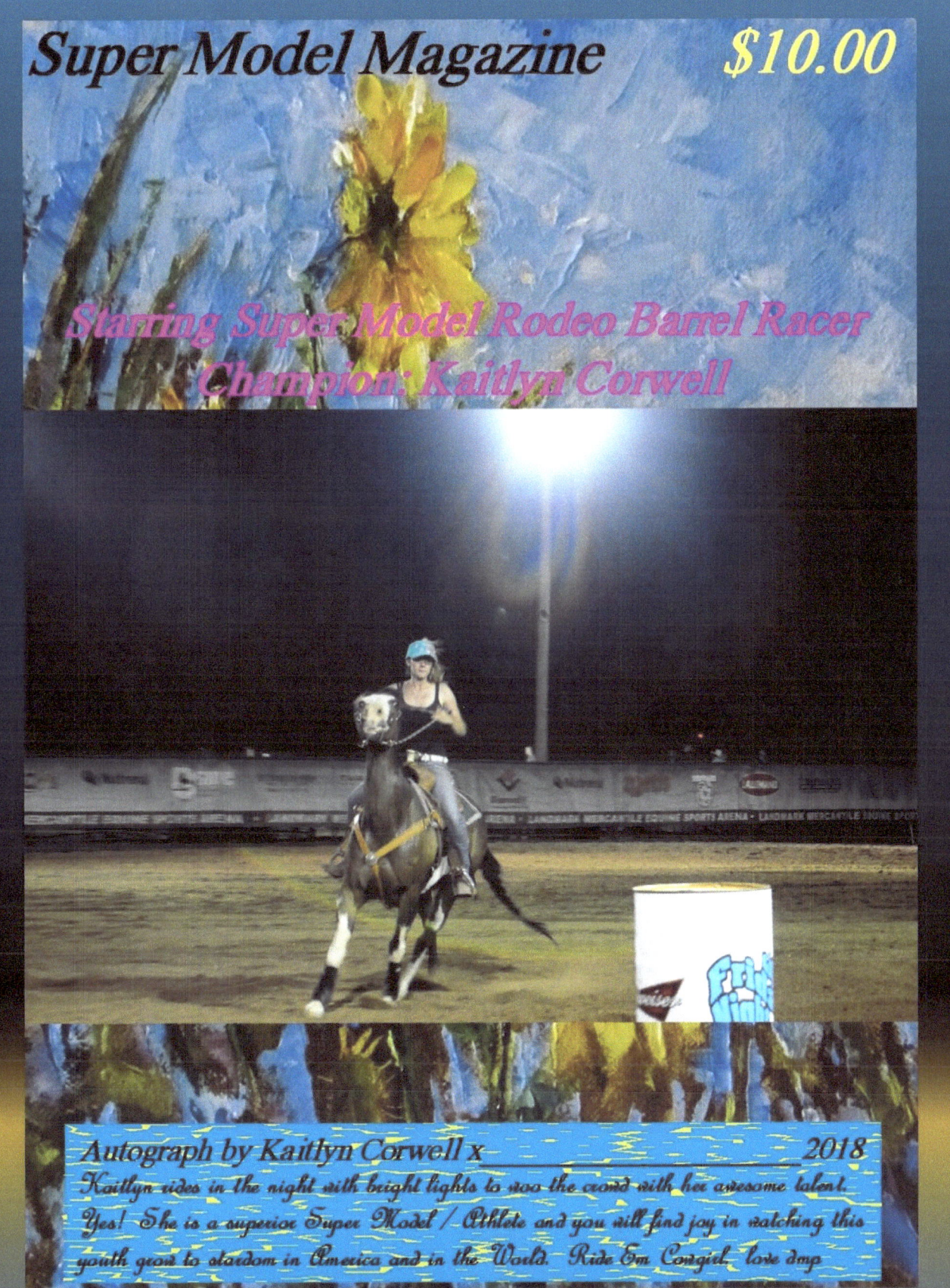

Autograph by Kaitlyn Corwell x   2018
Kaitlyn rides in the night with bright lights to wow the crowd with her awesome talent. Yes! She is a superior Super Model / Athlete and you will find joy in watching this youth grow to stardom in America and in the World. Ride Em Cowgirl. love dmp

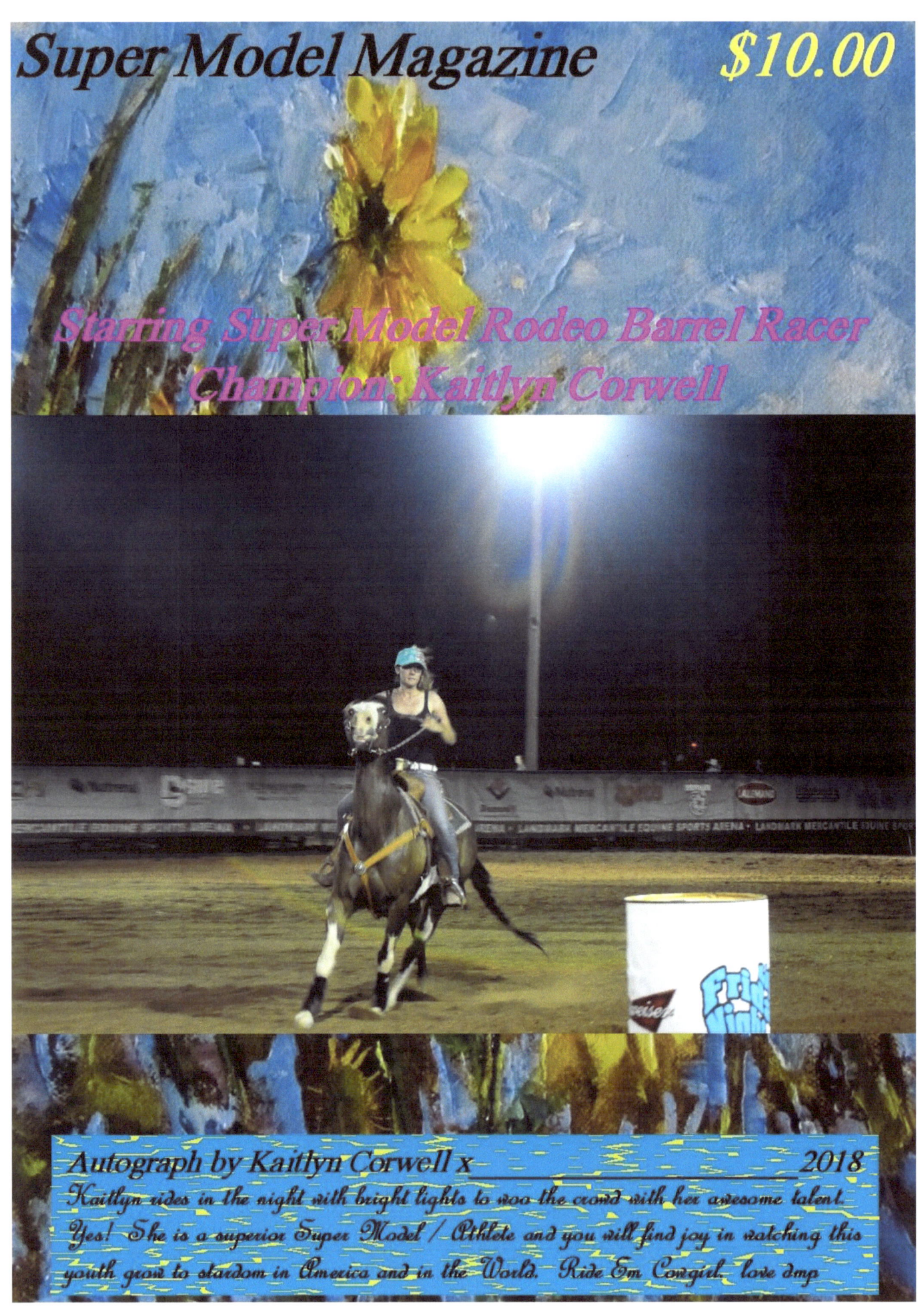

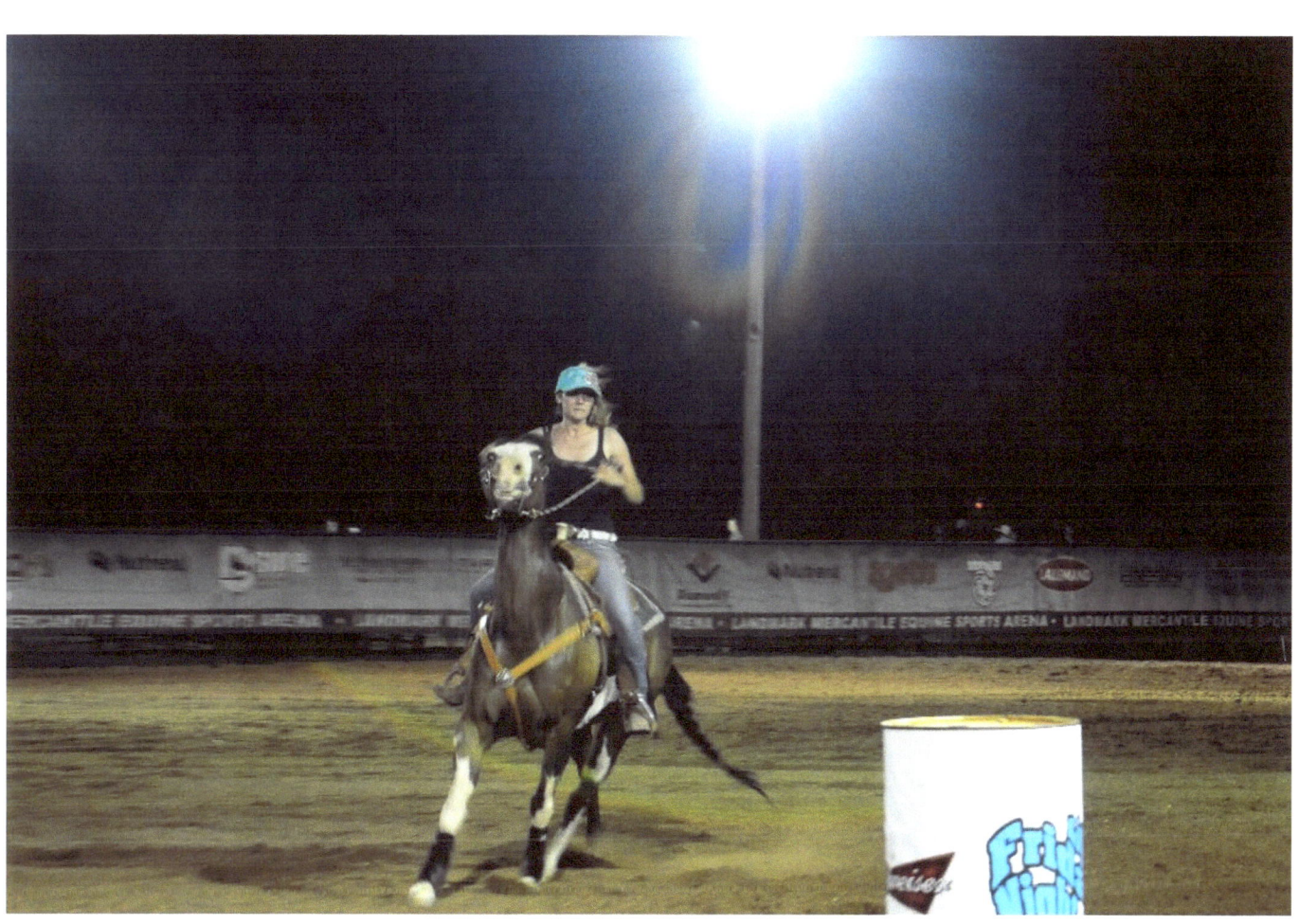

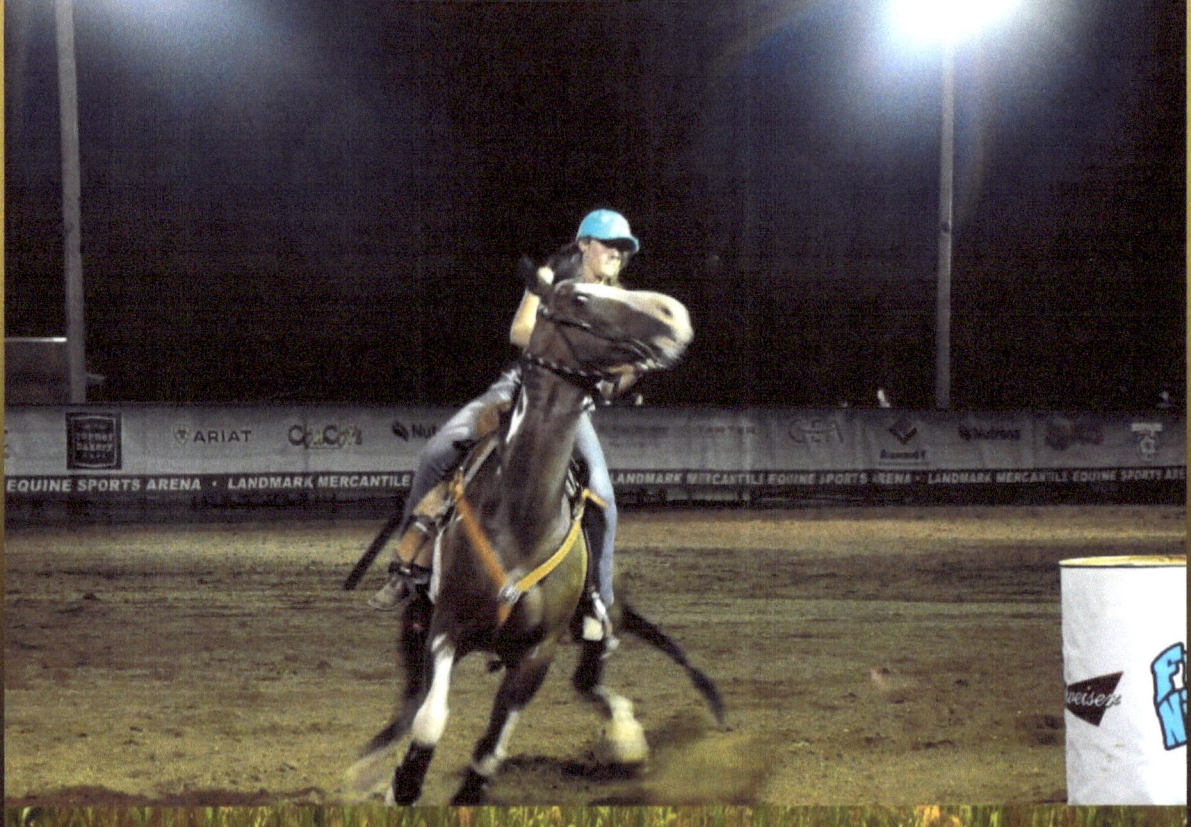

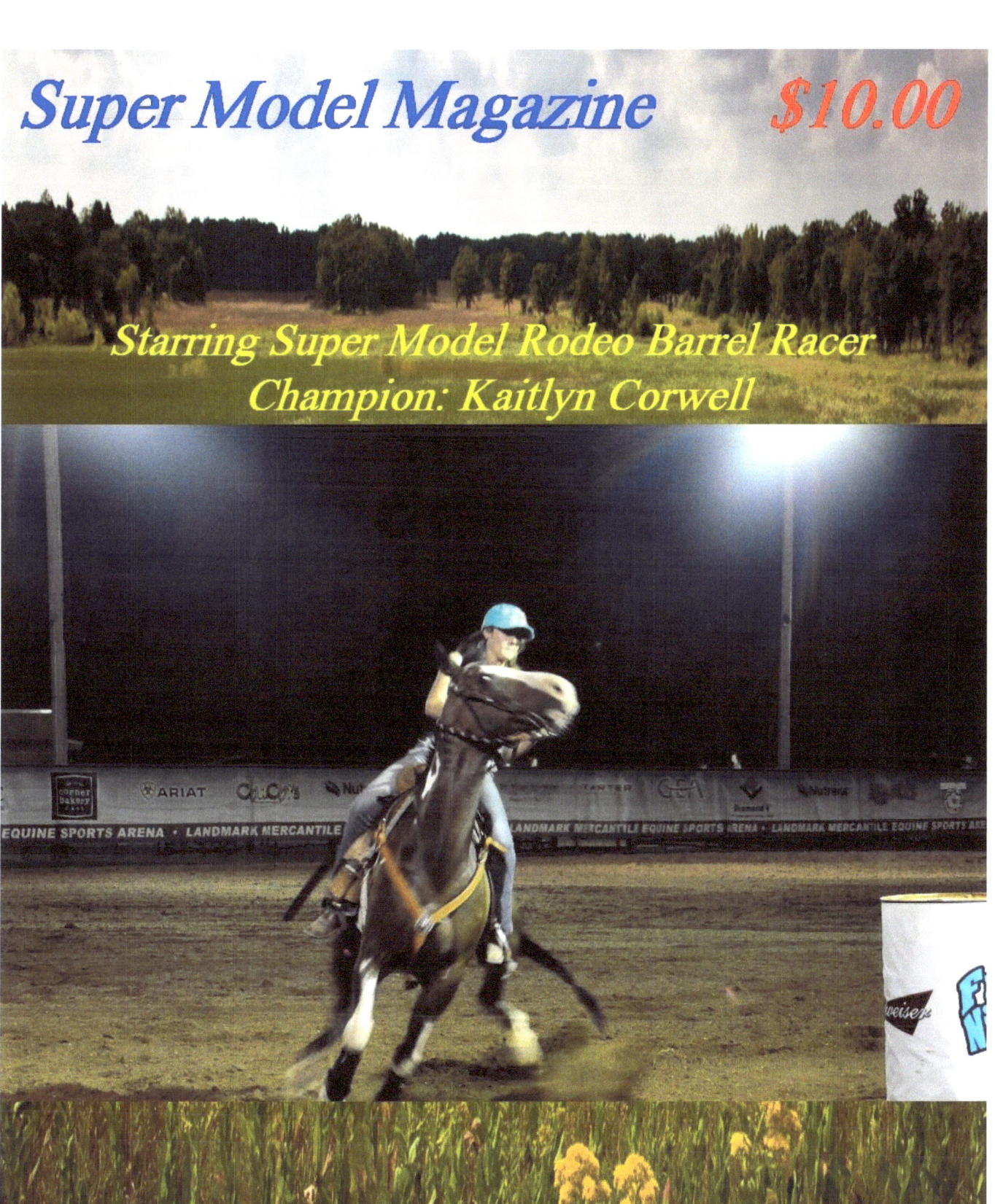

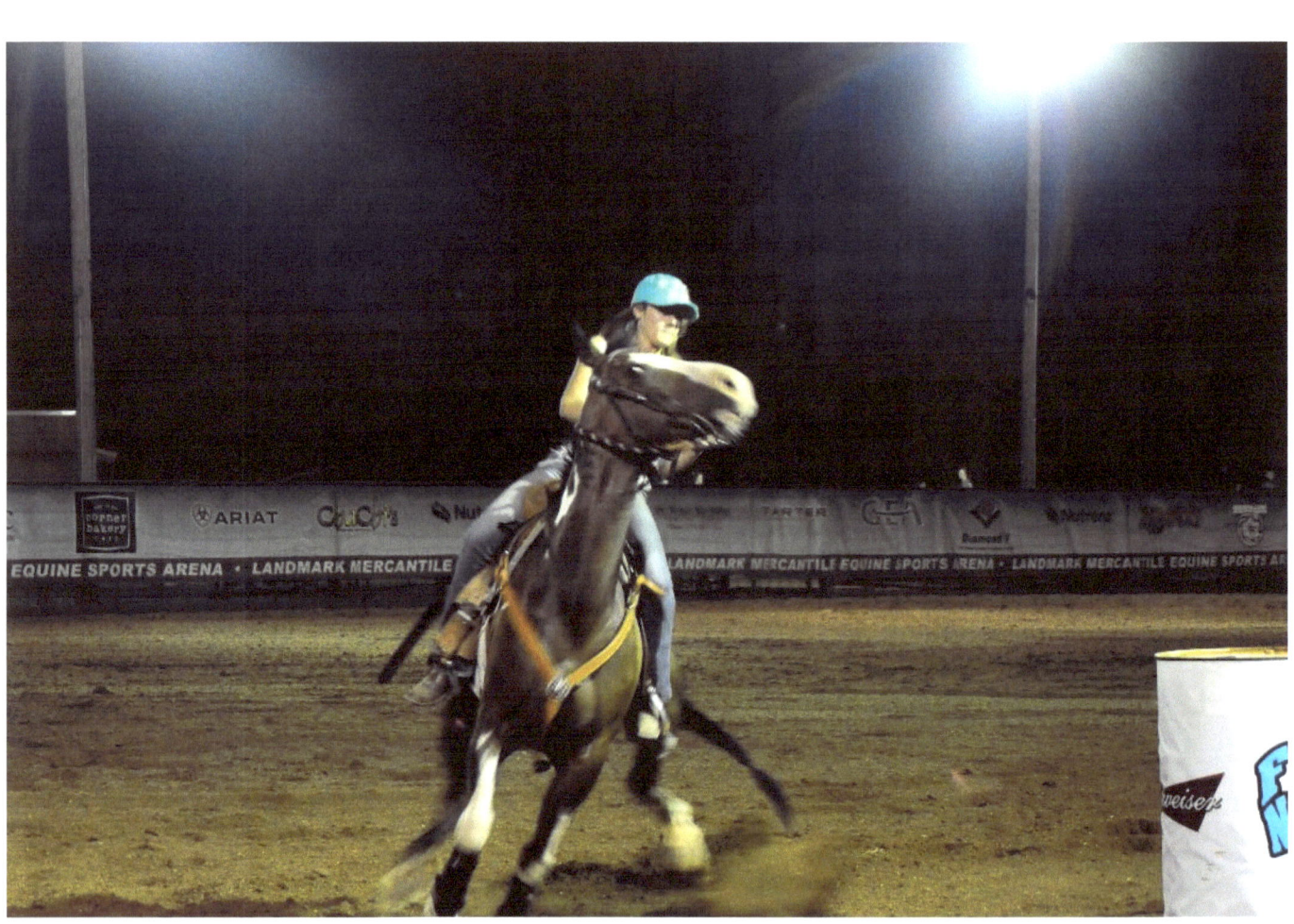

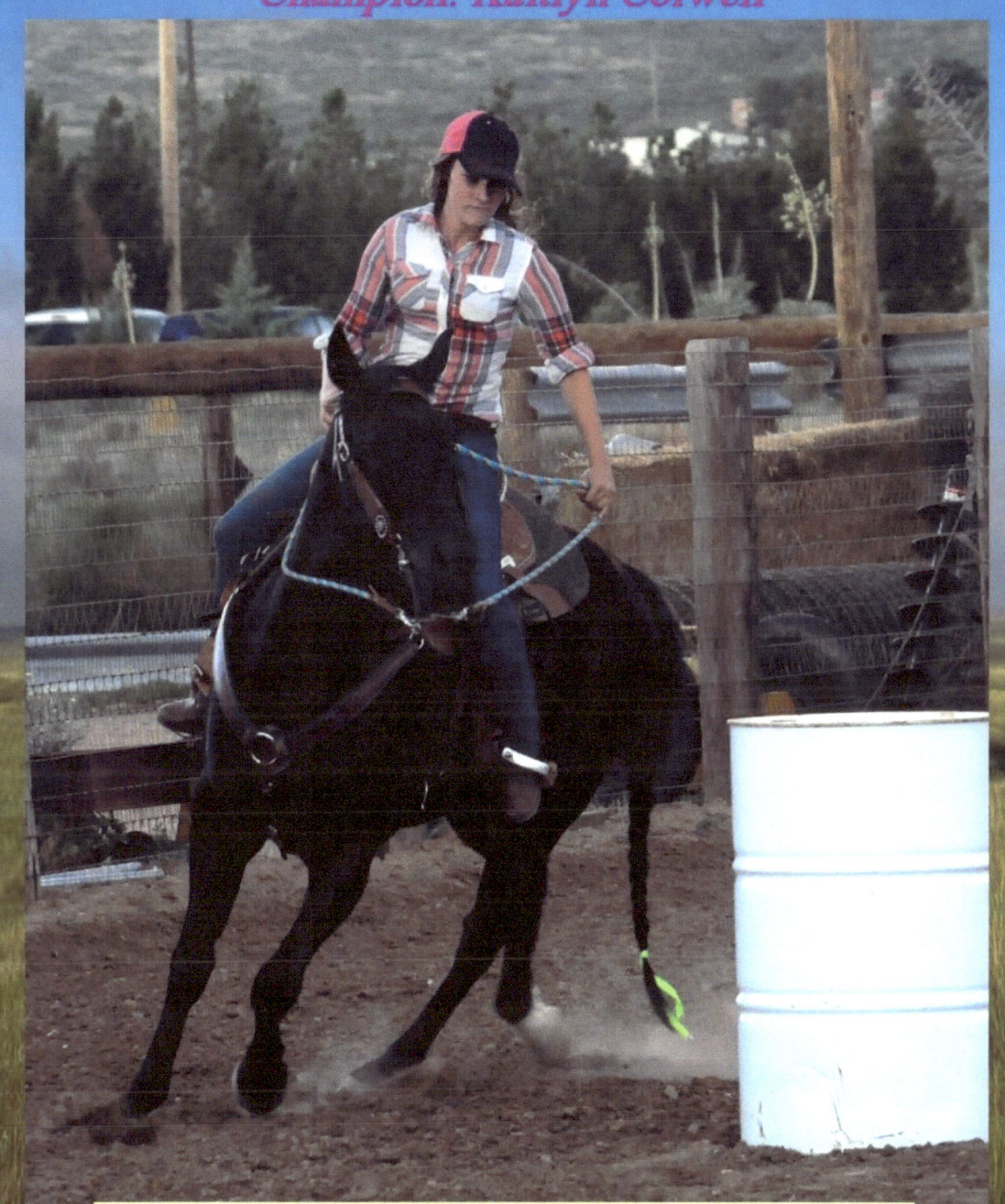

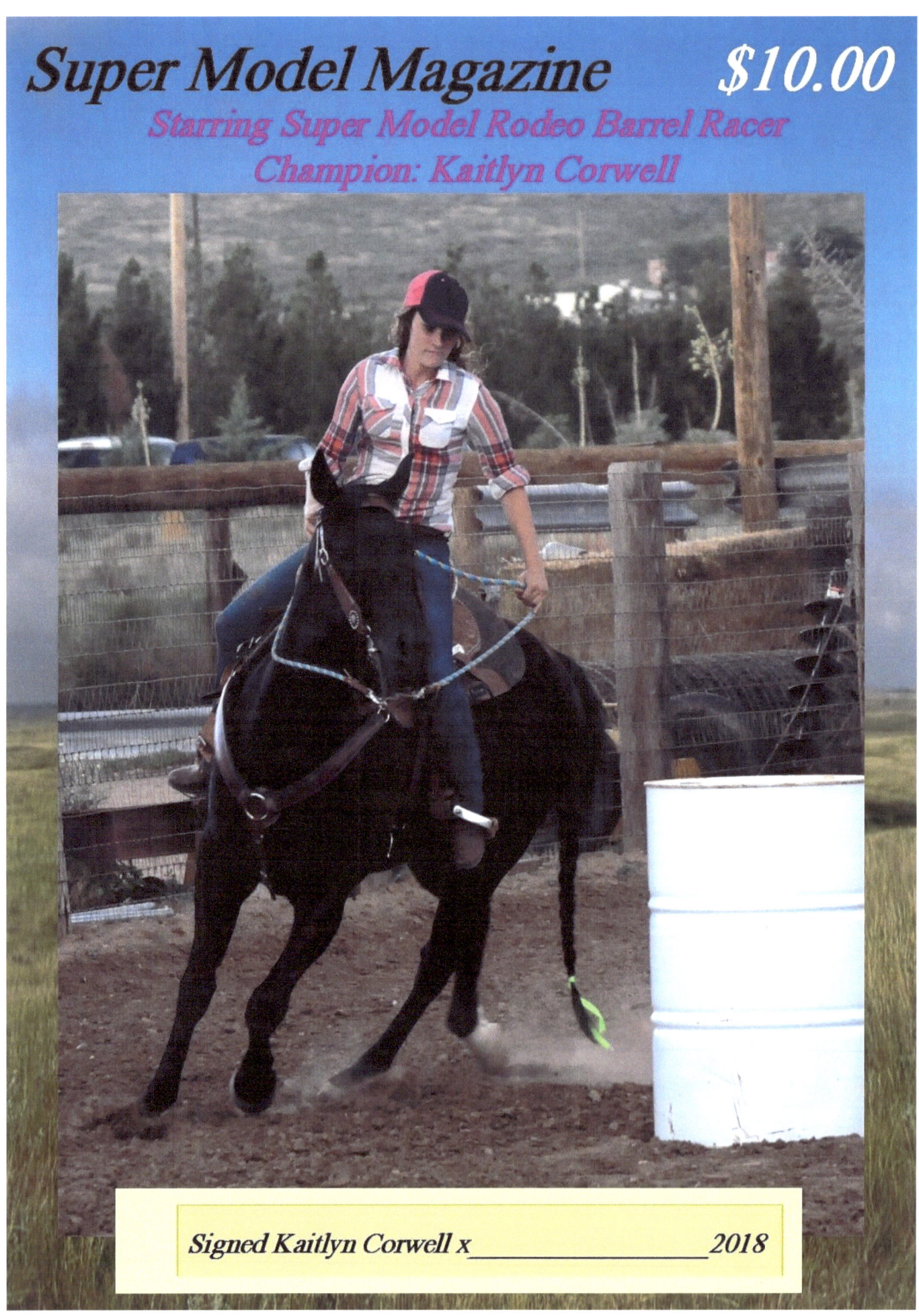

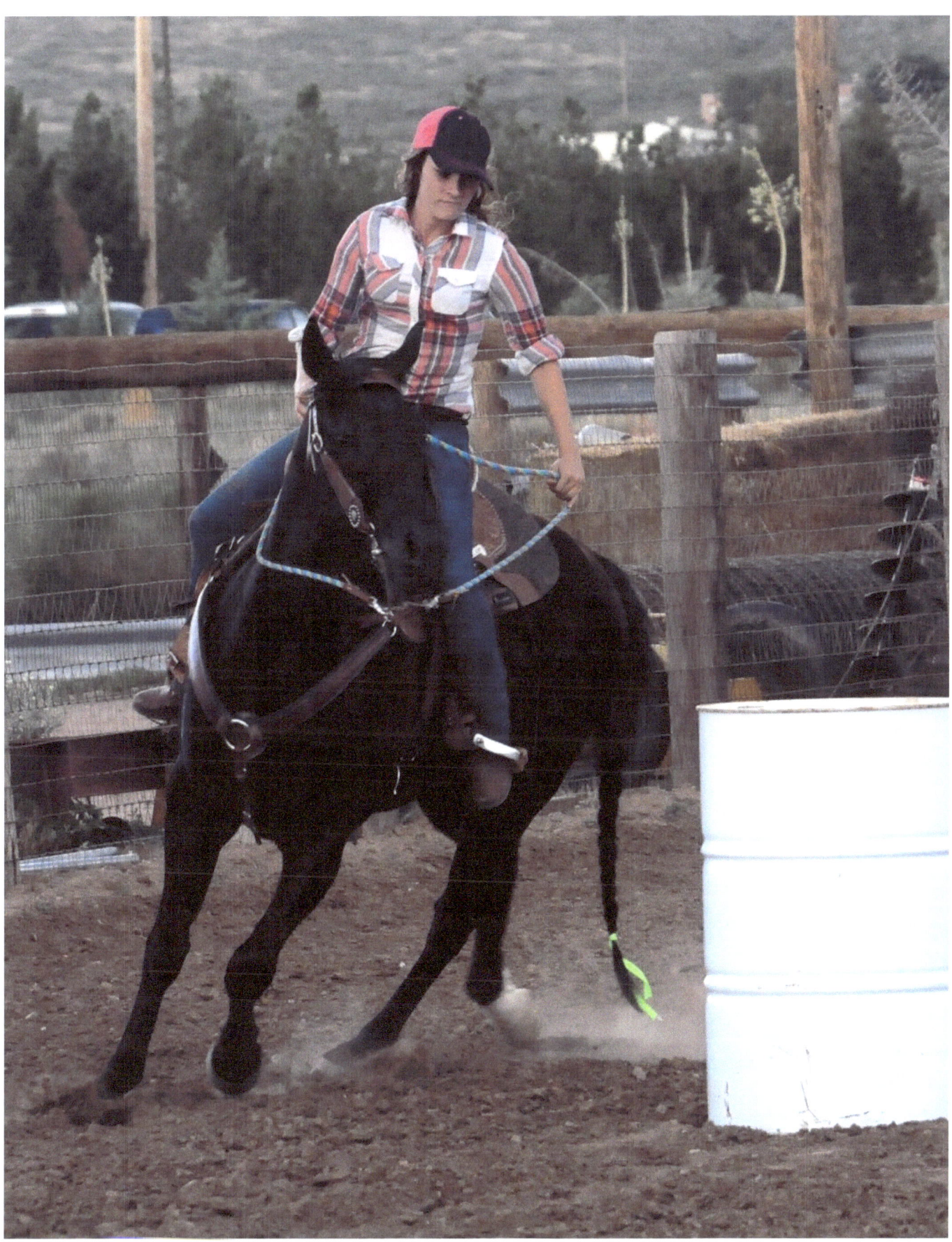

Super Model Magazine $10

Starring Super Model Rodeo Barrel Racing Champion: Kaitlin Corwell

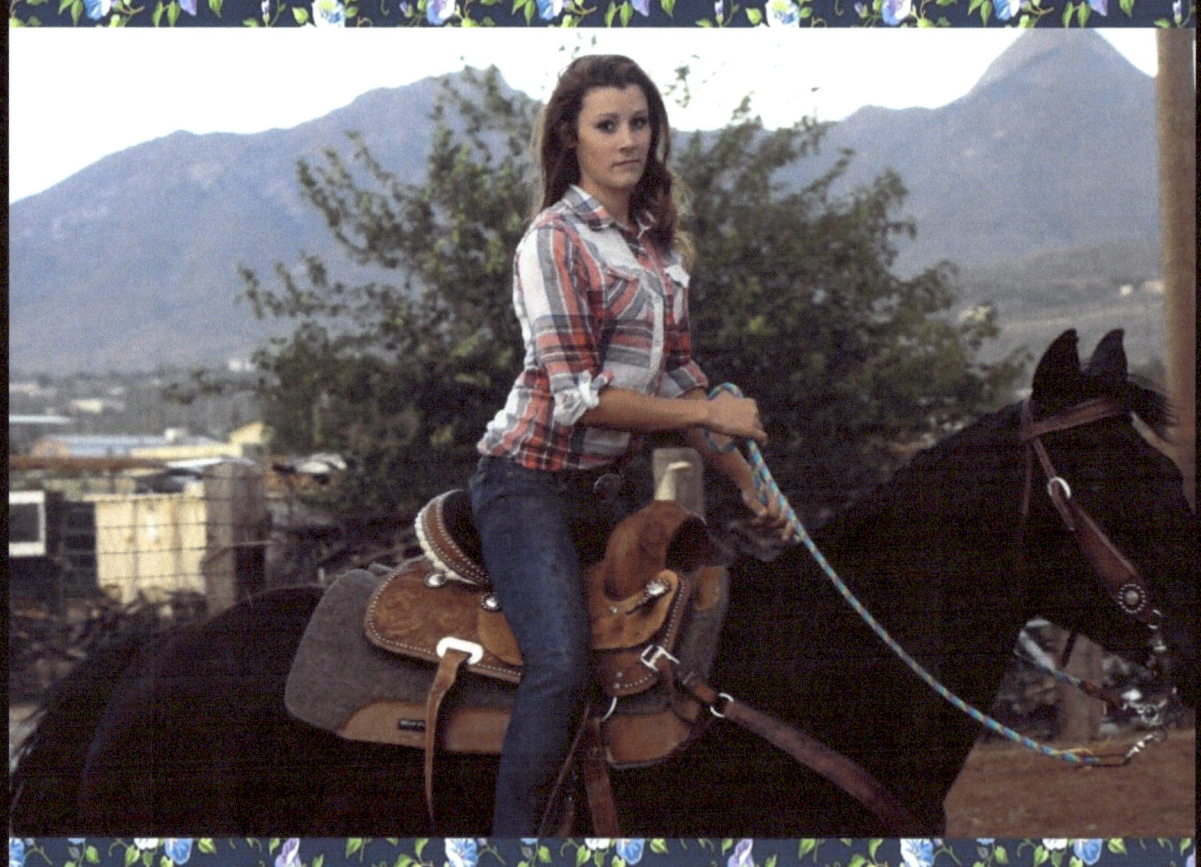

Signed Kaitlyn Corwell x_____ 2018

Super Model Magazine $10

Starring Super Model Rodeo Barrel Racing Champion: Kaitlin Corwell

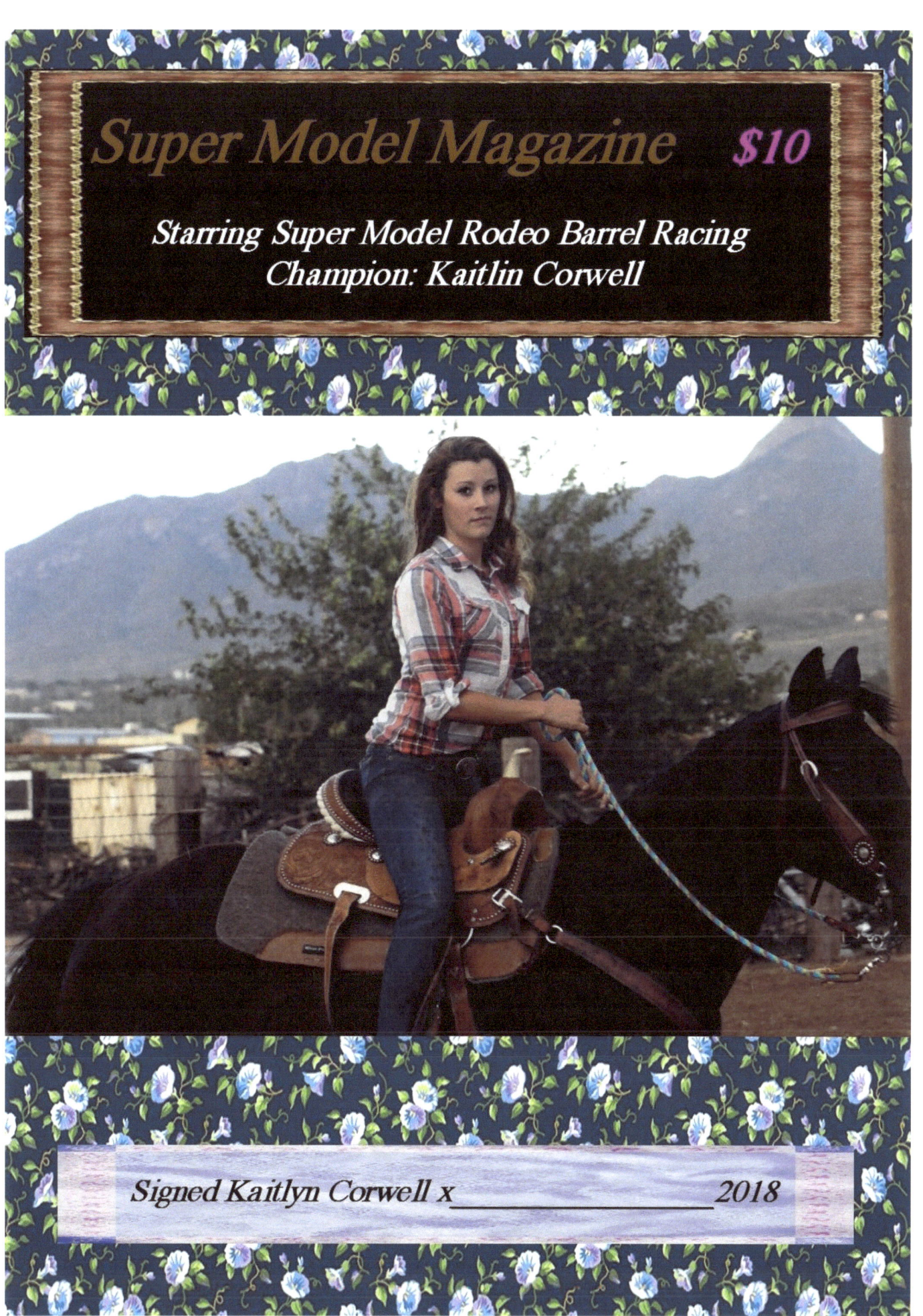

Signed Kaitlyn Corwell x_____ 2018

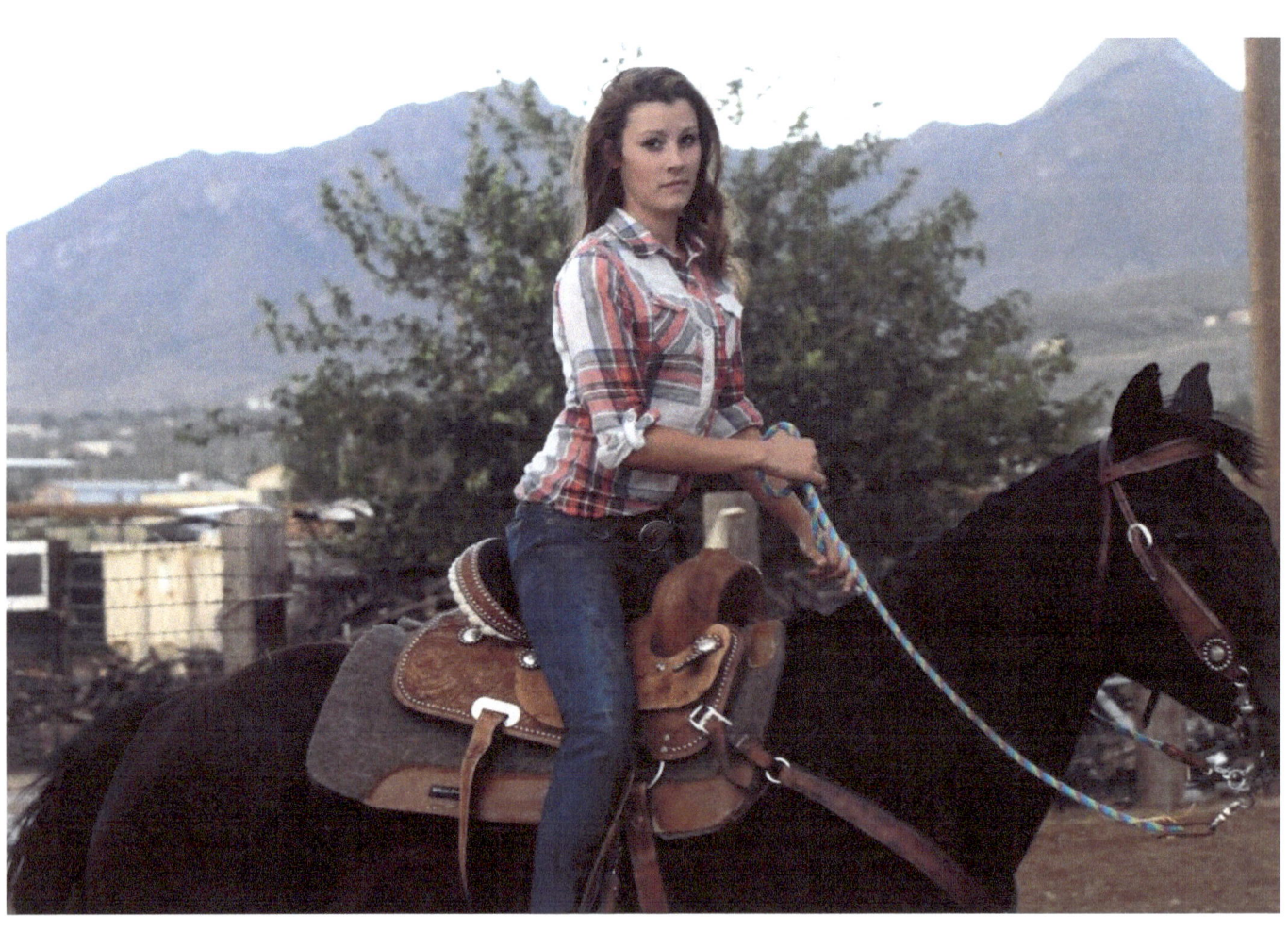

Super Model Magazine $10.00

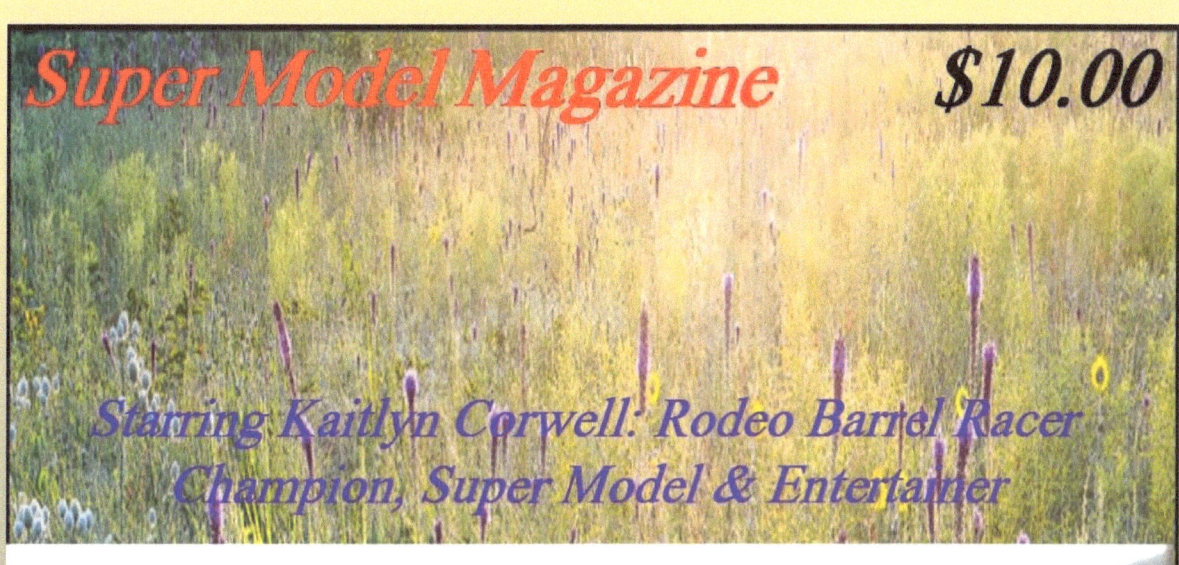

Starring Kaitlyn Corwell: Rodeo Barrel Racer Champion, Super Model & Entertainer

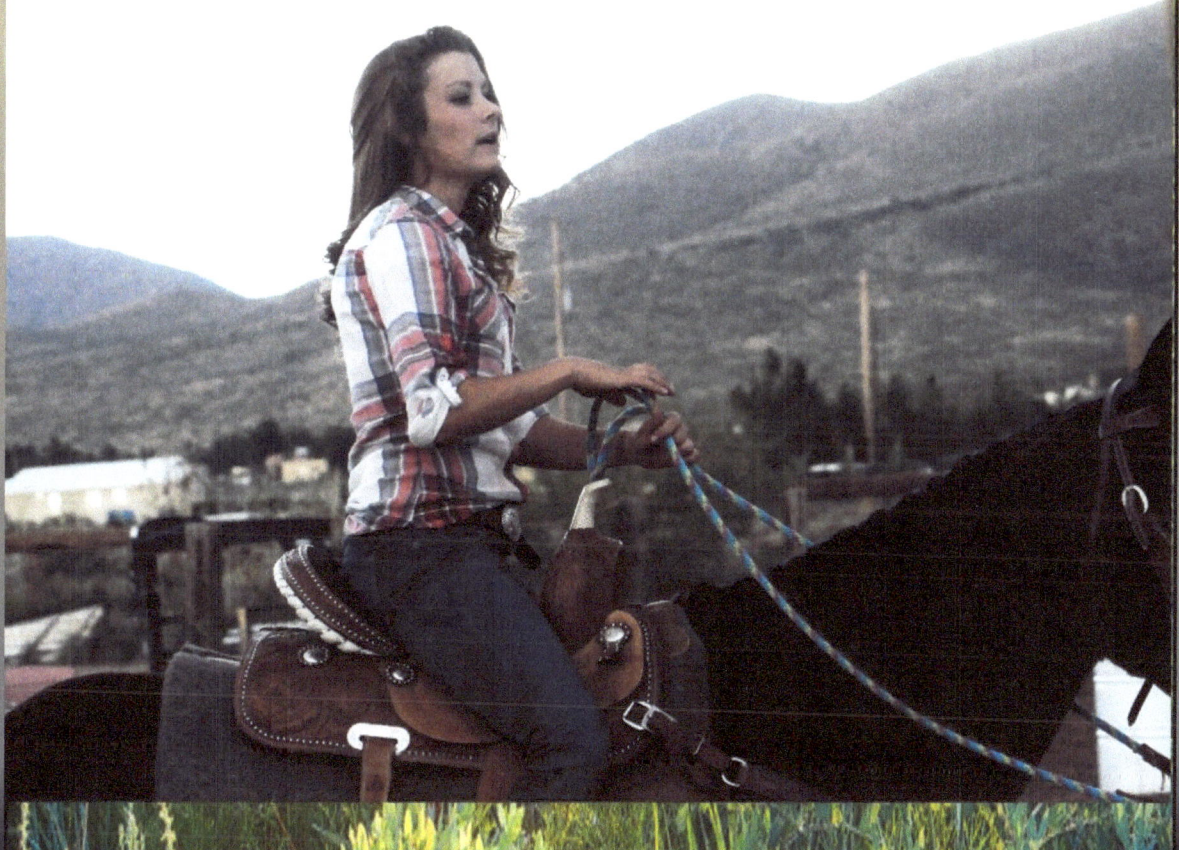

Love

Autograph by: Kaitlyn Corwell x_____ 2018

Kaitlyn Corwell is a profession that prances her way to success and stardom as a Super Model and Actress avant guarde. She's beautiful ann ever so becoming, that puts on showmanship, like none other horse racing athlete. Ride Em Cowgirl. dmp

Super Model Magazine $10.00

Starring Kaitlyn Corwell: Rodeo Barrel Racer Champion, Super Model & Entertainer

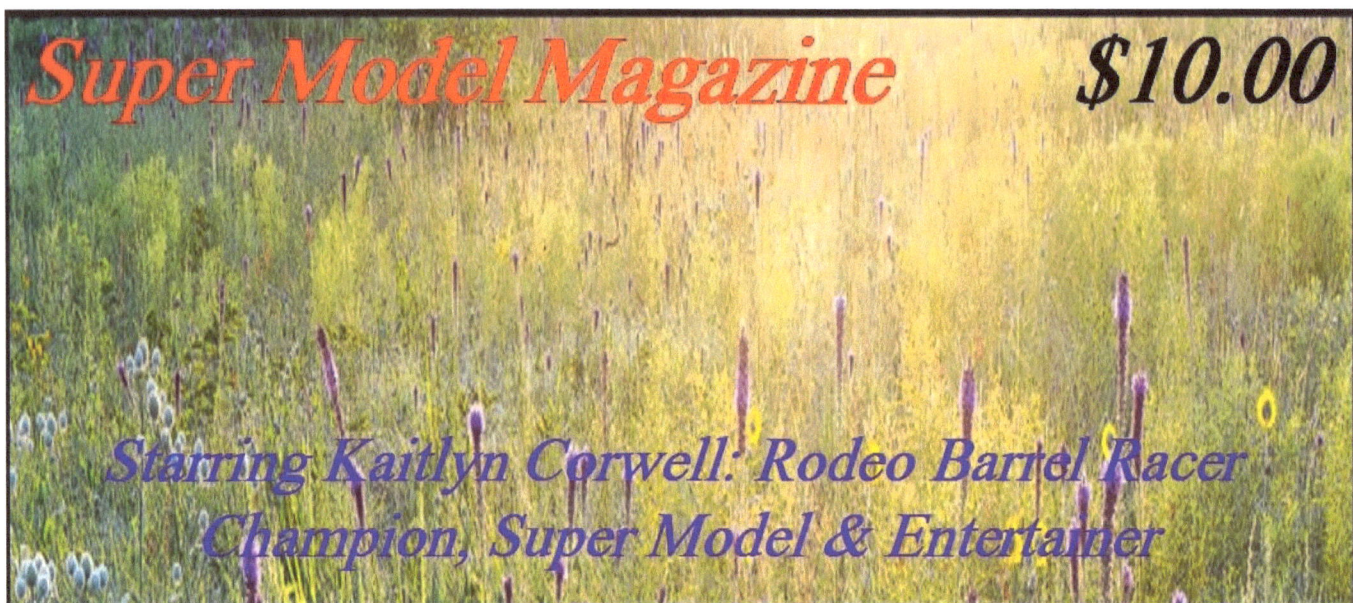

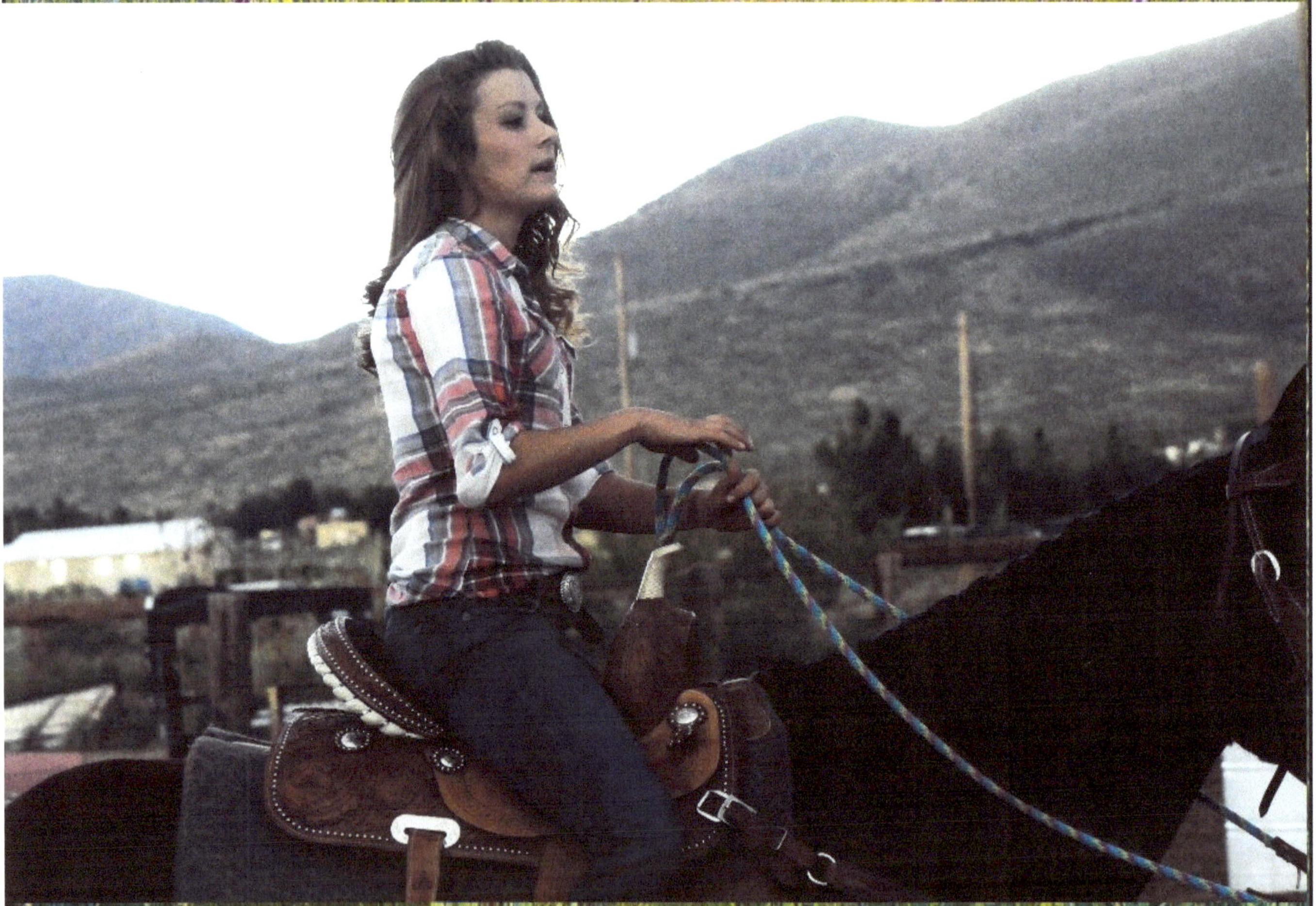

L o v e

Autograph by: Kaitlyn Corwell x_____ 2018

Kaitlyn Corwell is a profession that prances her way to success and stardom as a Super Model and Actress avant guarde. She's beautiful ann ever so becoming, that puts on showmanship, like none other horse racing athlete. Ride Em Cowgirl. dmp

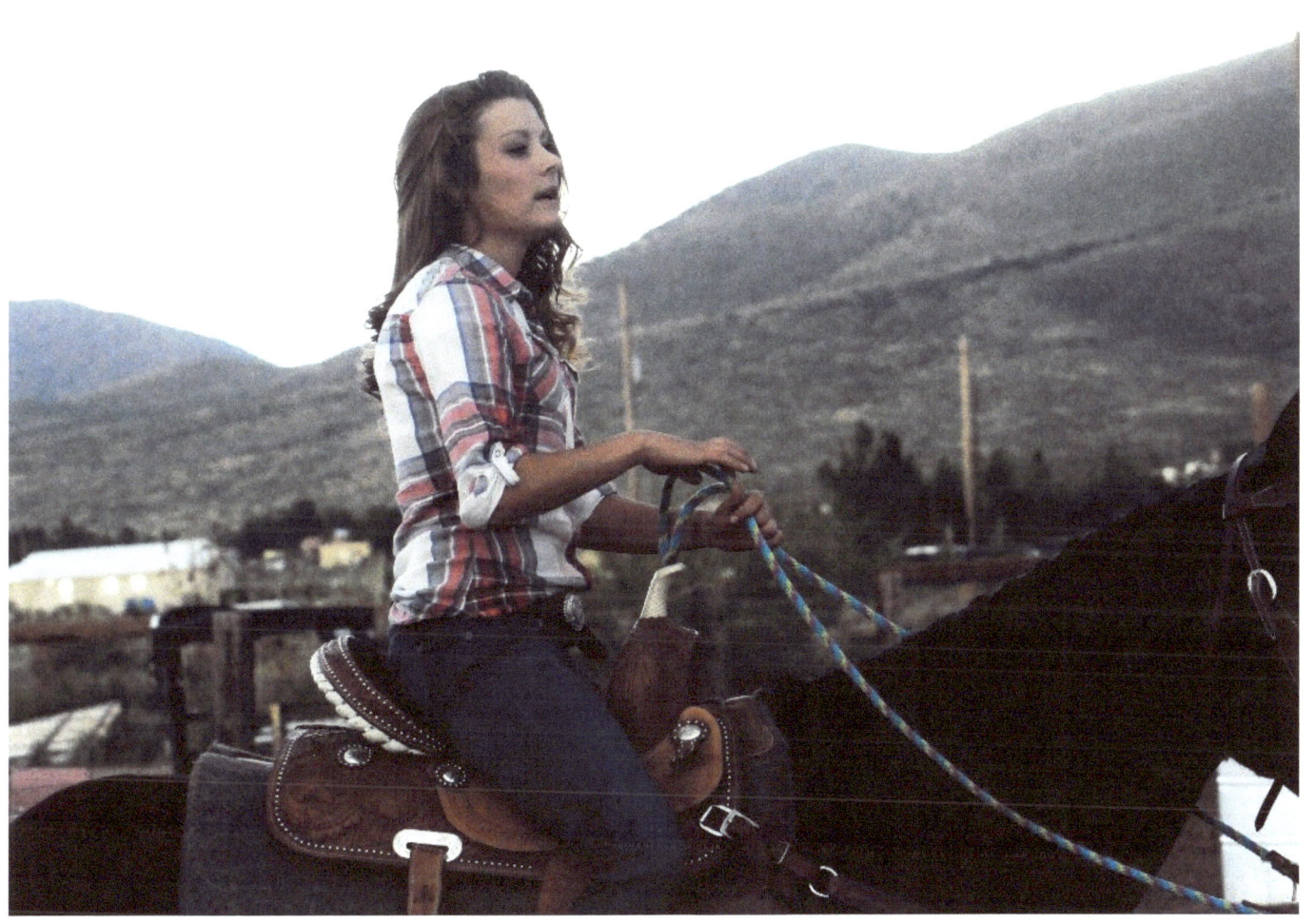

Super Model Magazine $10.00

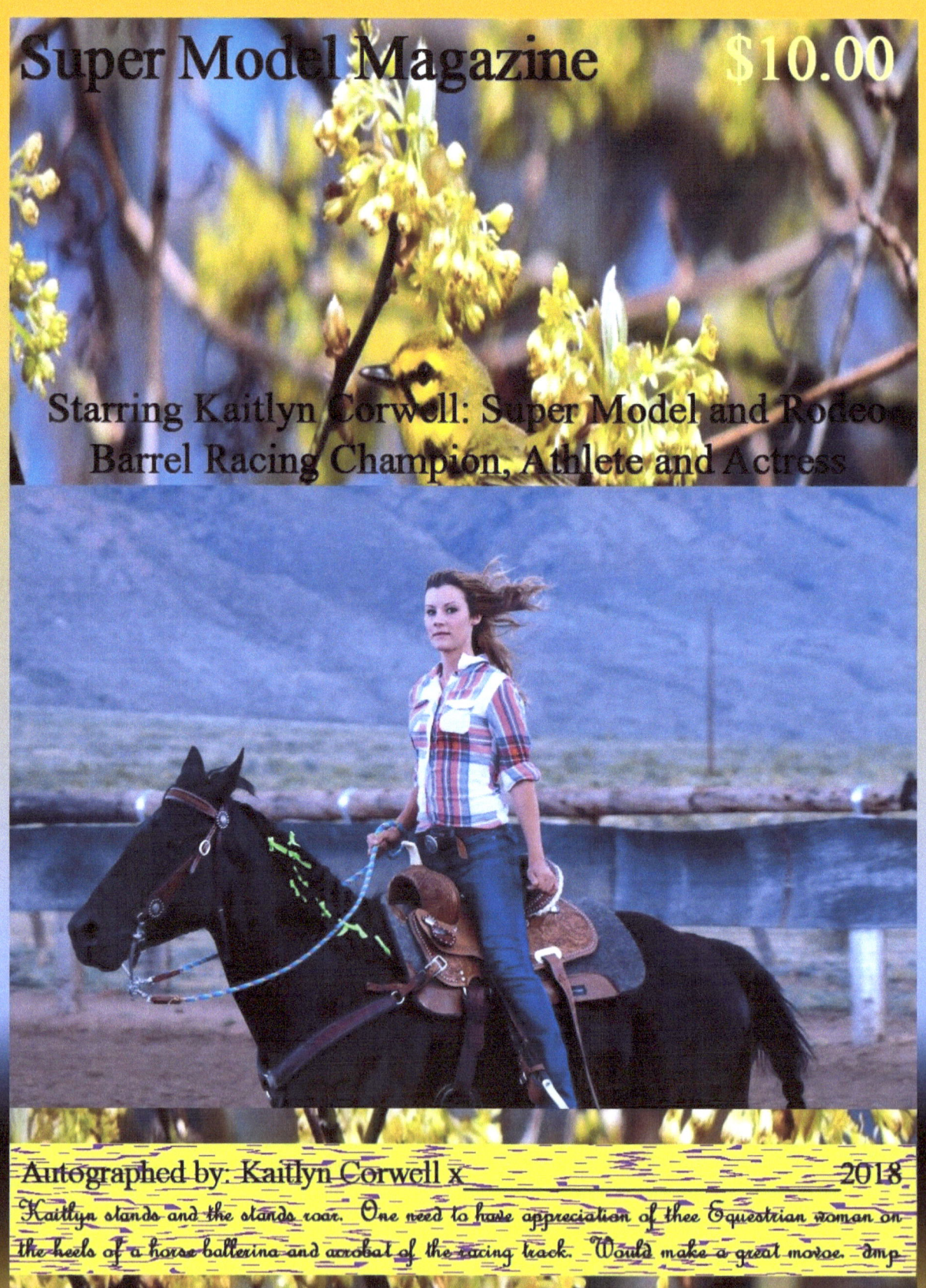

Starring Kaitlyn Corwell: Super Model and Rodeo Barrel Racing Champion, Athlete and Actress

Autographed by: Kaitlyn Corwell x _____ 2018

Kaitlyn stands and the stands roar. One need to have appreciation of thee Equestrian woman on the heels of a horse ballerina and acrobat of the racing track. Would make a great movie. smp

Super Model Magazine $10.00

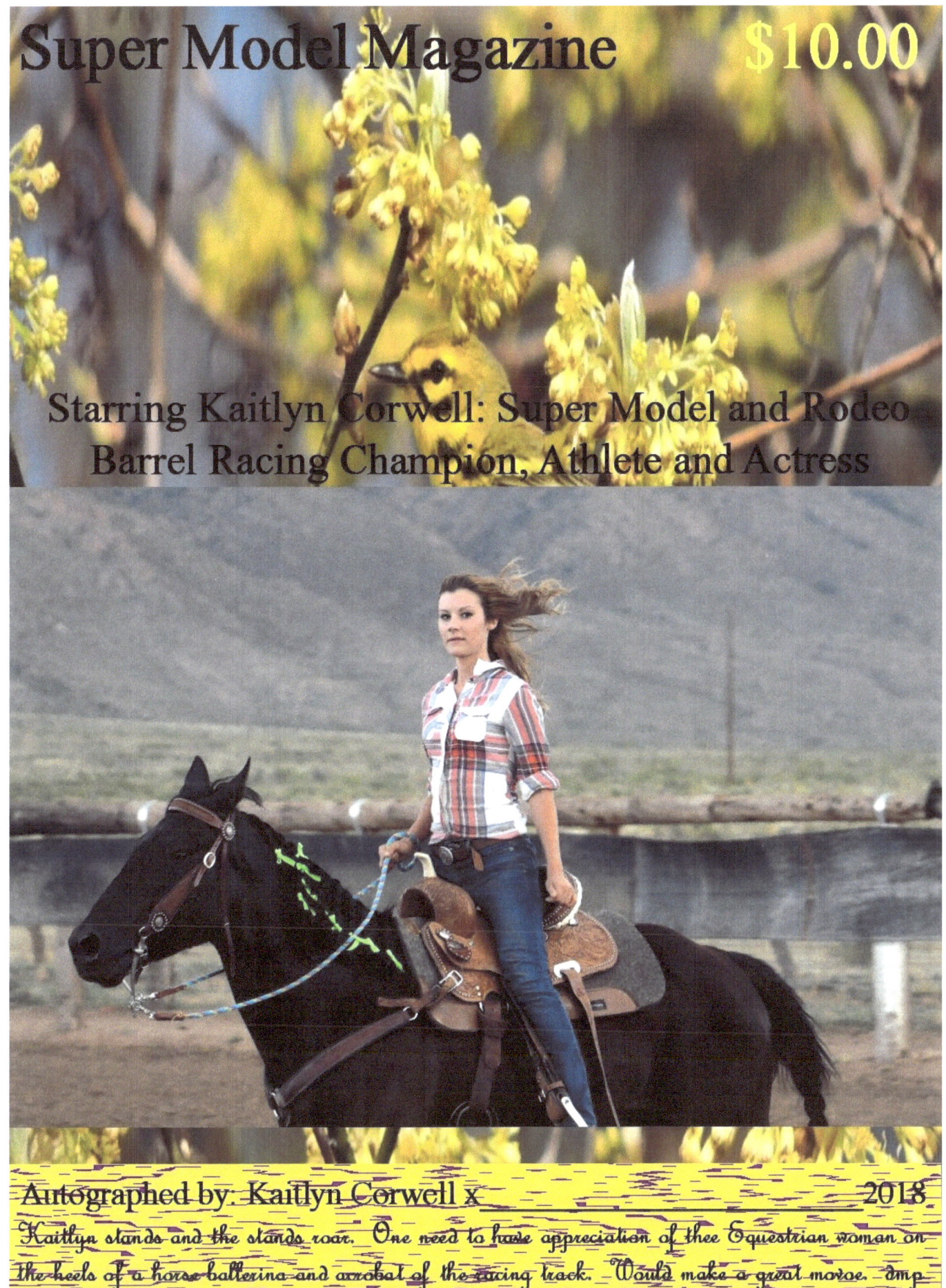

Starring Kaitlyn Corwell: Super Model and Rodeo Barrel Racing Champion, Athlete and Actress

Autographed by: Kaitlyn Corwell x _____ 2018

Kaitlyn stands and the stands roar. One need to have appreciation of thee Equestrian woman on the heels of a horse ballerina and acrobat of the racing track. Would make a great movie. amp

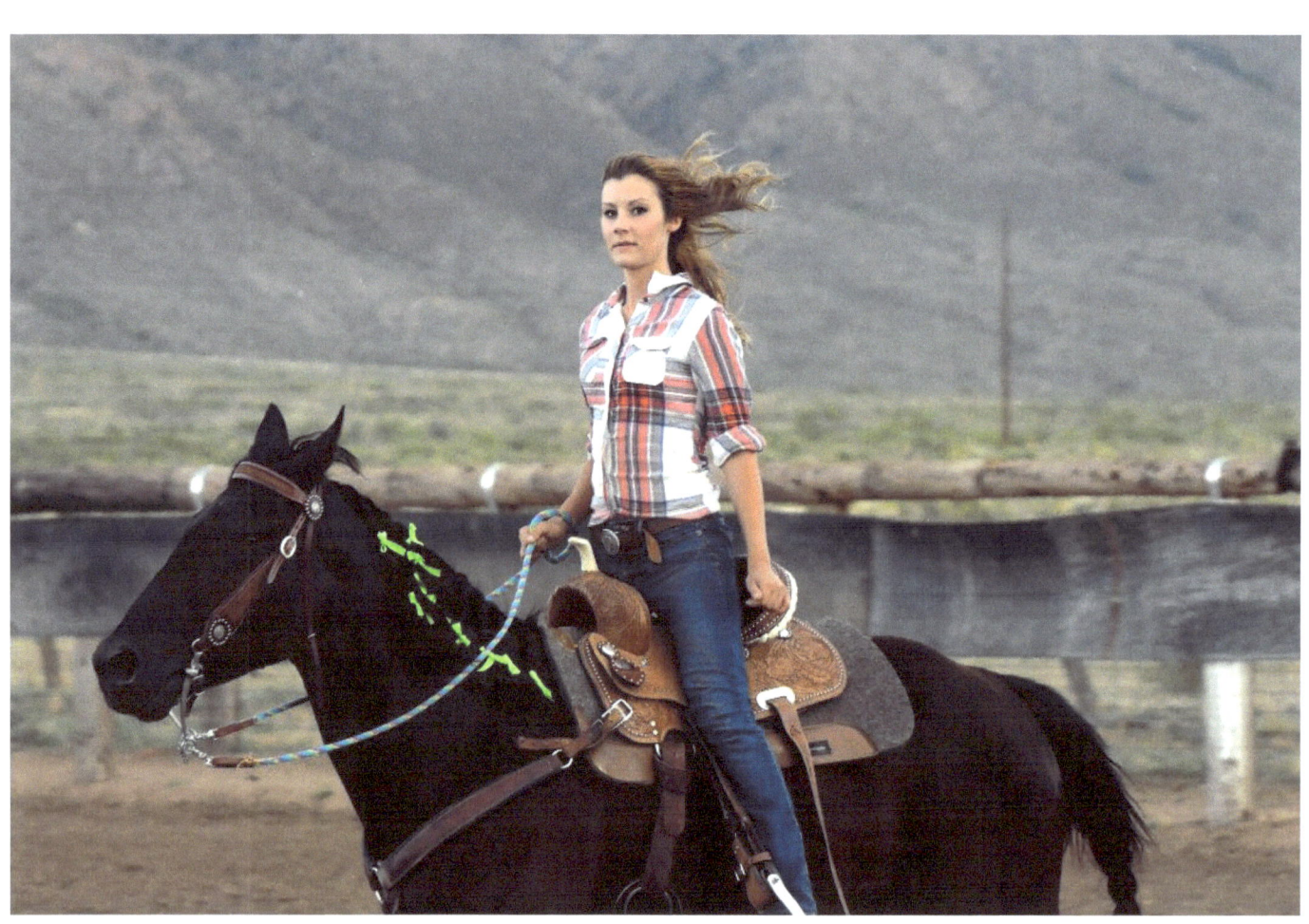

Super Model Magazine $10.00

Starring Kaitlyn Corwell: Super Model & Rodeo Barrel Racing Champion. Athlete and Entertainer.

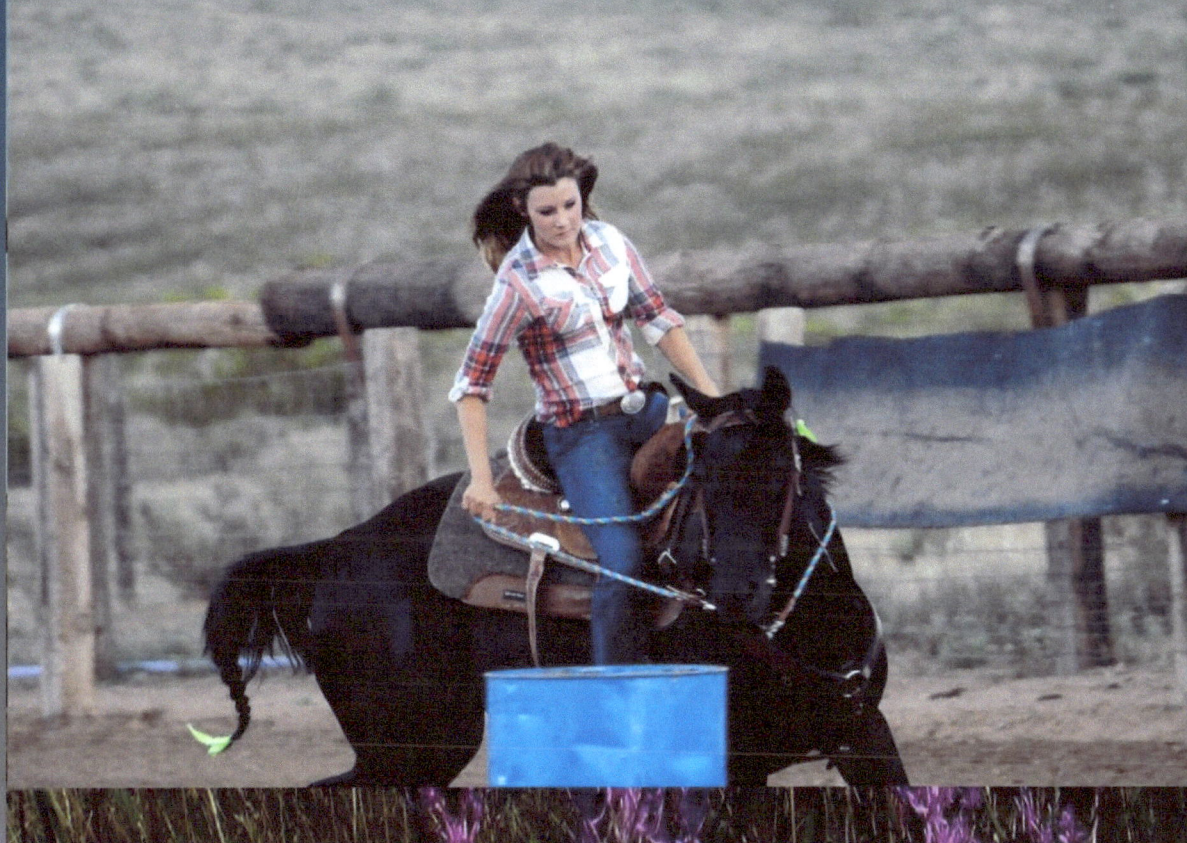

Signed by: Kaitlyn Corwell x_____ 2018

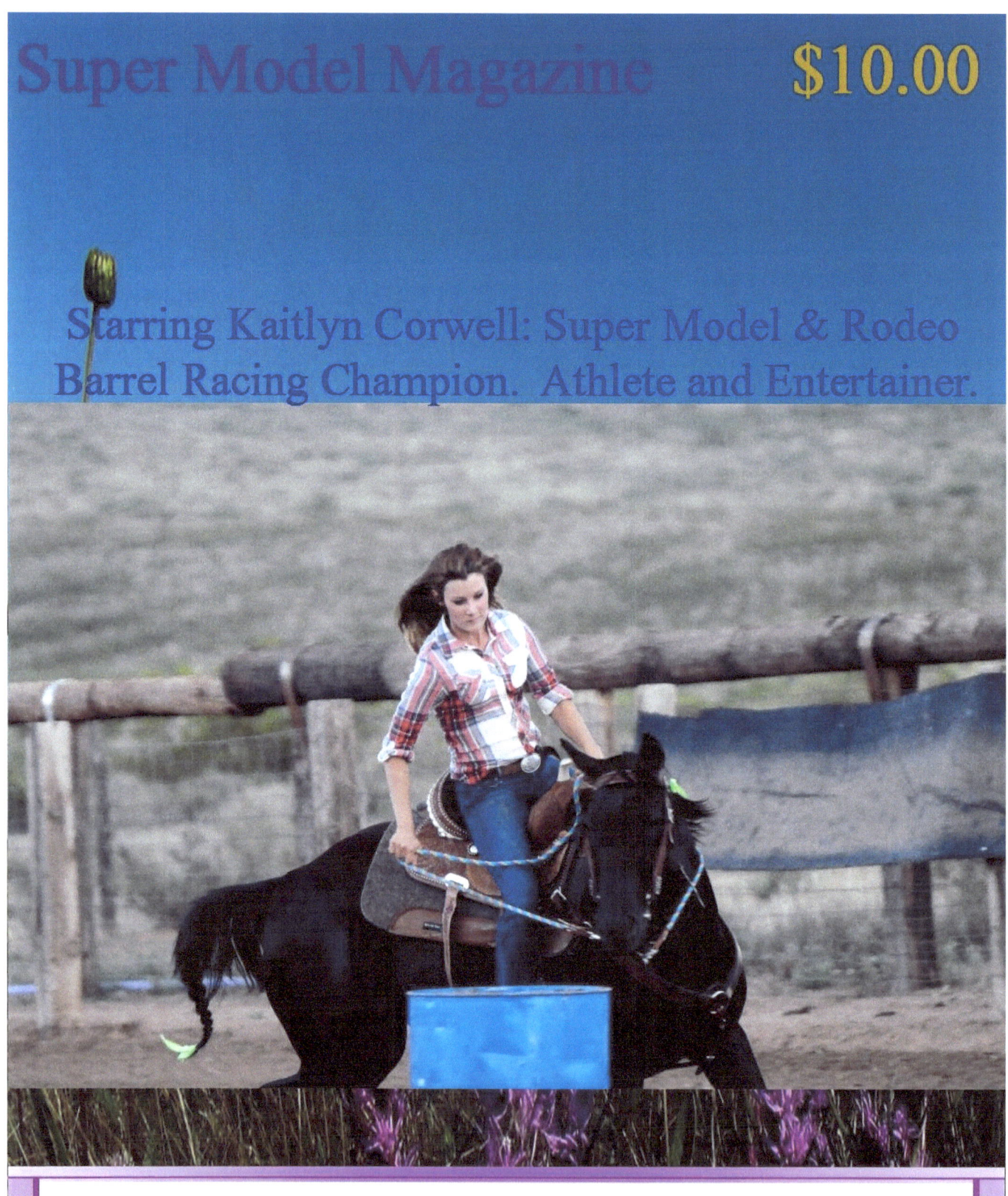

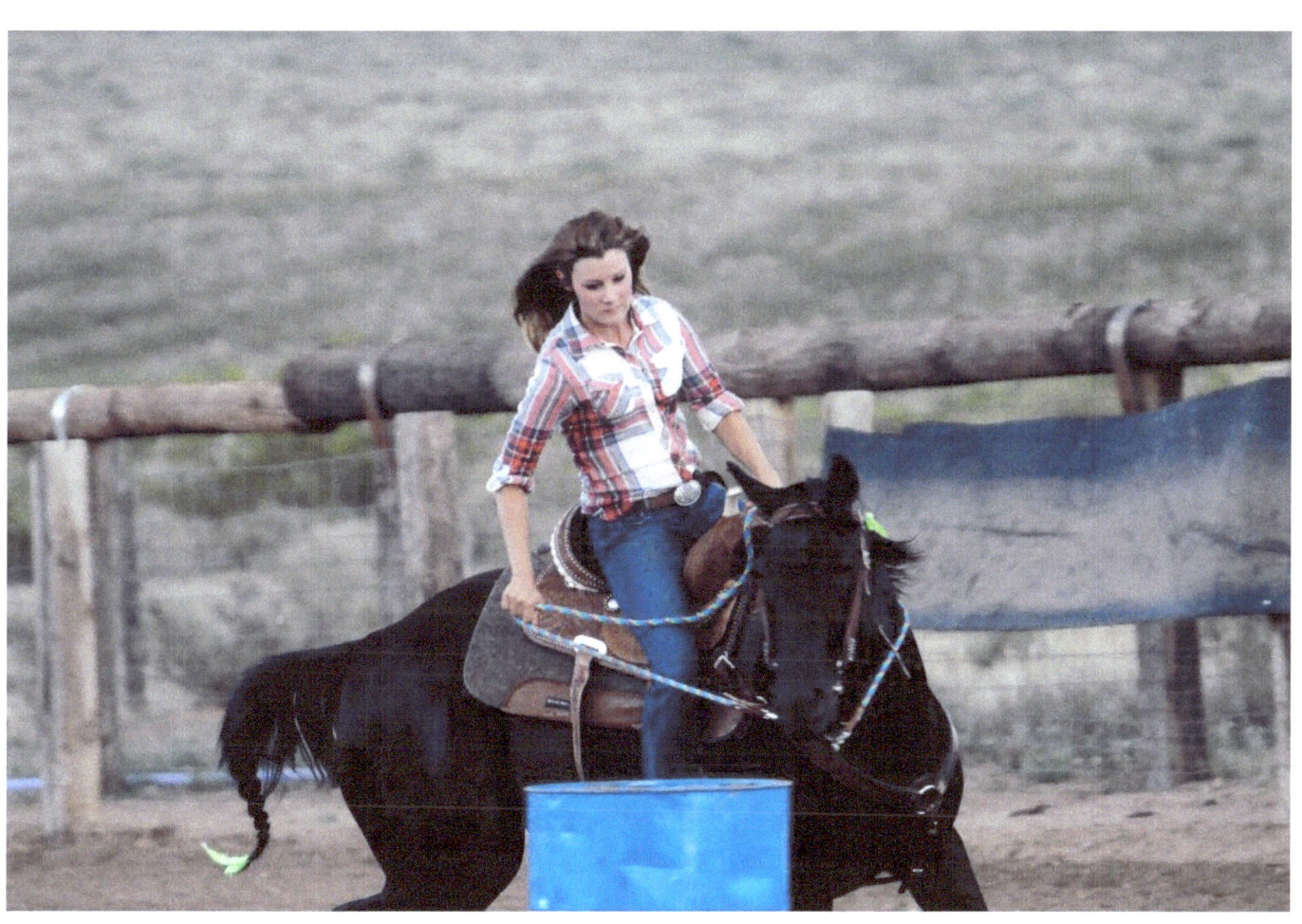

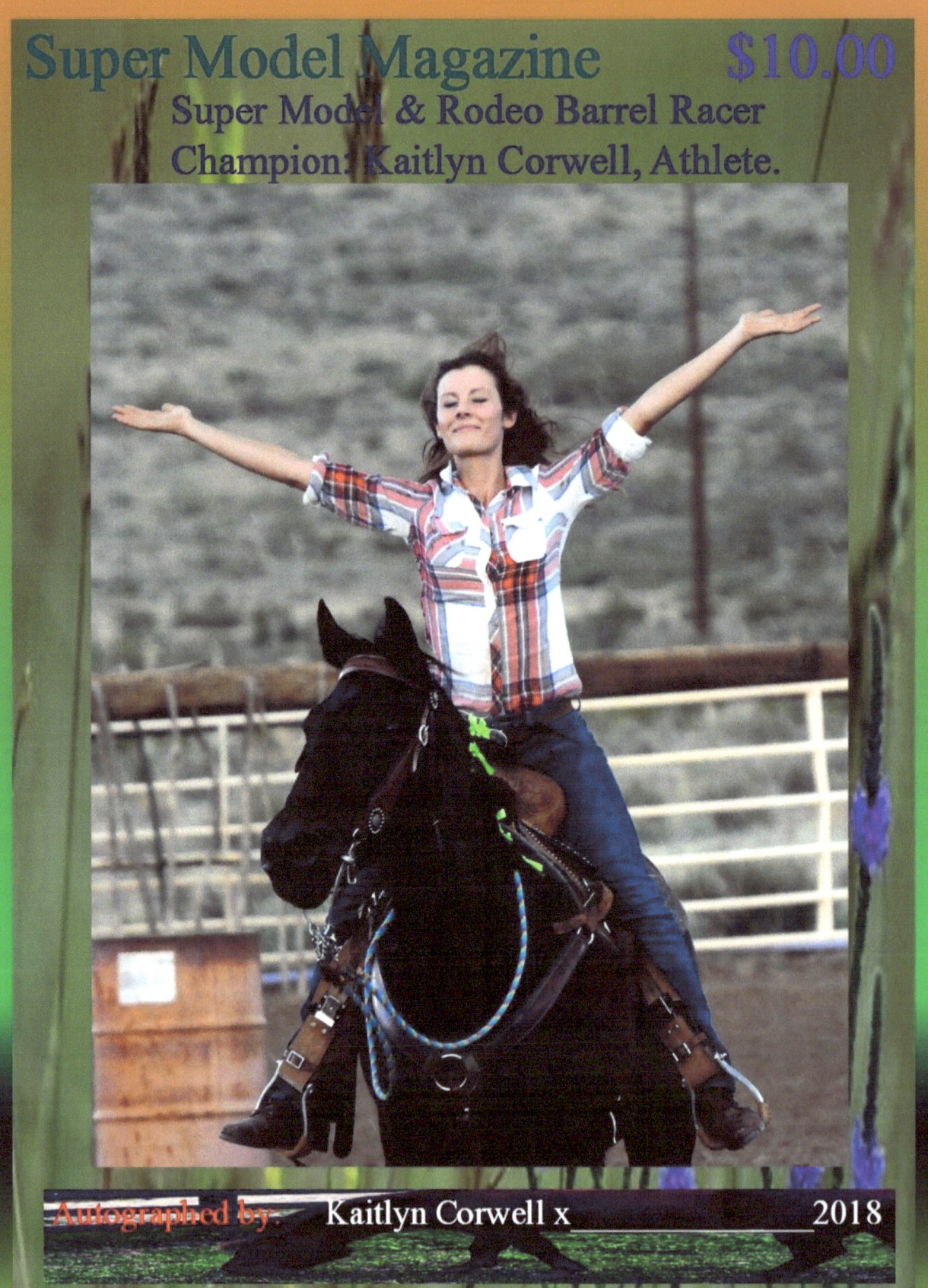

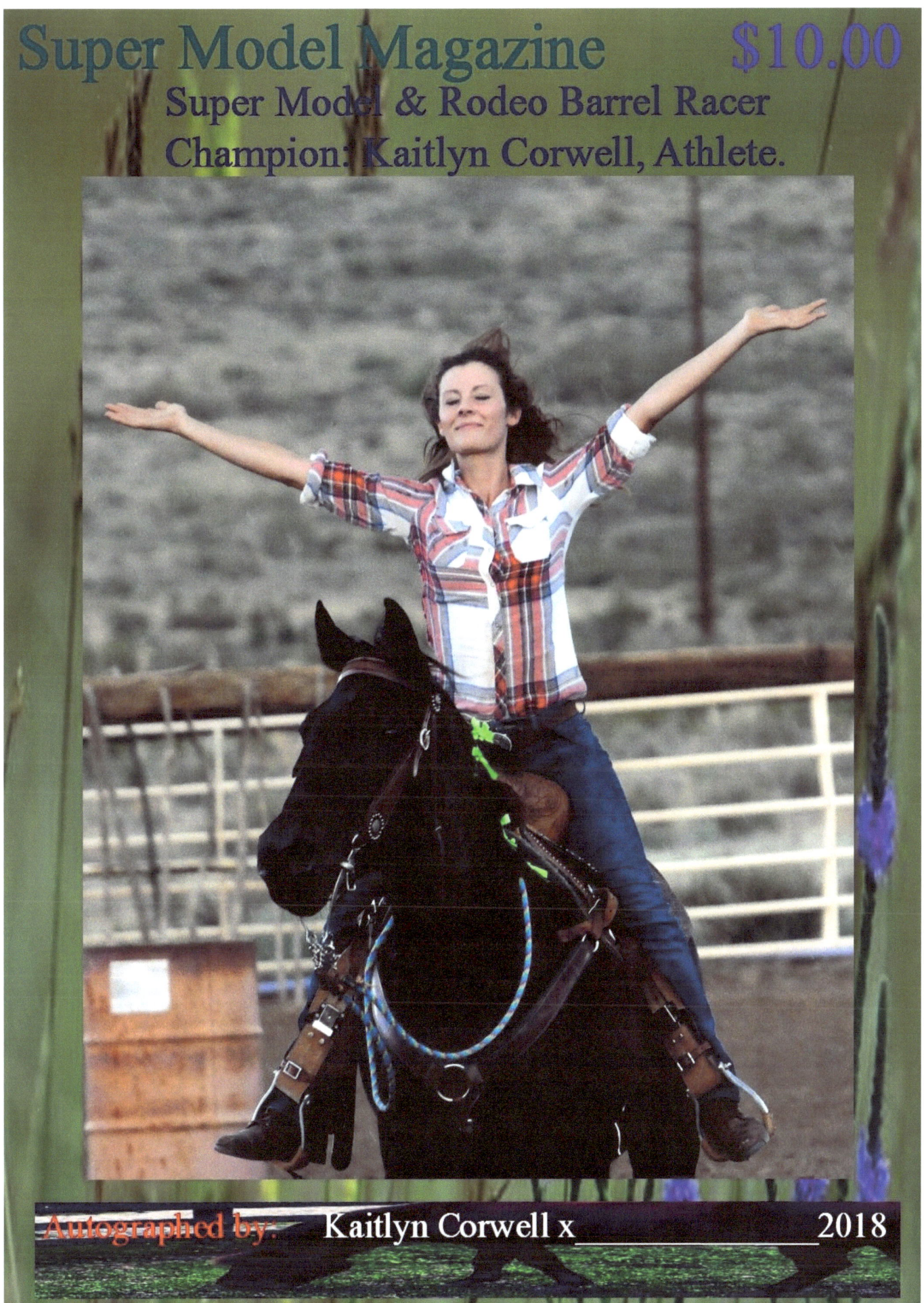

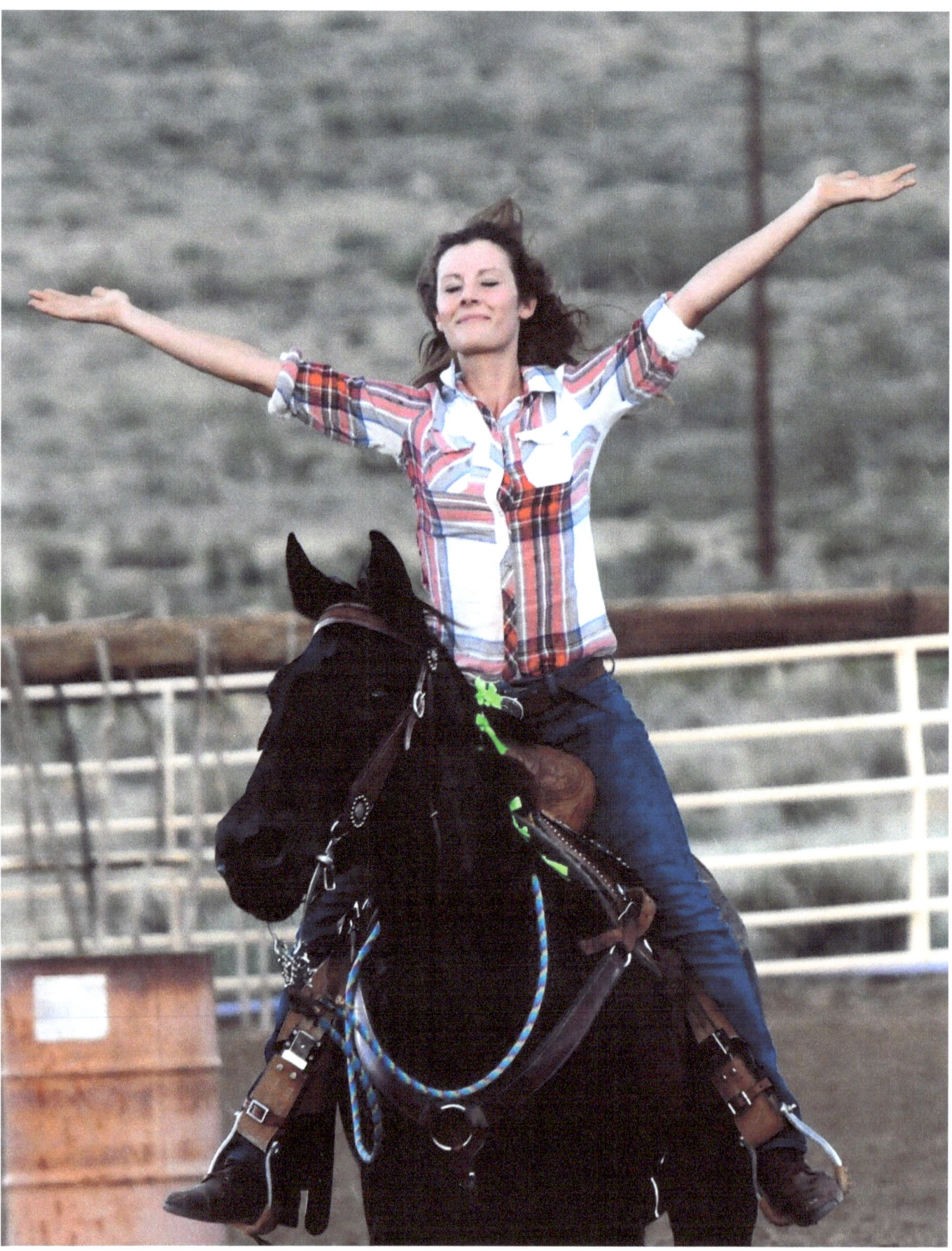

www.ingramcontent.com/pod-product-compliance
Lightning Source LLC
Chambersburg PA
CBHW040453220526
45473CB00004B/1616